Harwood Fundamentals of Pure and Applied Economics

MARKET STRUCTURE AND PERFORMANCE

FUNDAMENTALS OF PURE AND APPLIED ECONOMICS

INDUSTRIAL ECONOMICS I
In 3 Volumes

I	Dynamic Models of Oligopoly	*Fudenberg and Tirole*
II	The Corporation	*Mueller*
III	Market Structure and Performance	*Cubbin*

MARKET STRUCTURE AND PERFORMANCE

The Empirical Research

JOHN S CUBBIN

ROUTLEDGE
Taylor & Francis Group

First published in 1988 by
Harwood Academic Publishers GmbH

Reprinted in 2001 by
Routledge

2 Park Square, Milton Park, Abingdon, Oxfordshire OX14 4RN
711 Third Avenue, New York, NY 10017

First issued in paperback 2014

Routledge is an imprint of the Taylor & Francis Group, an informa business

The publishers have made every effort to contact authors/copyright holders of the works reprinted in *Harwood Fundamentals of Pure & Applied Economics*. This has not been possible in every case, however, and we would welcome correspondence from those individuals/companies we have been unable to trace.

These reprints are taken from original copies of each book. in many cases the condition of these originals is not perfect. the publisher has gone to great lengths to ensure the quality of these reprints, but wishes to point out that certain characteristics of the original copies will, of necessity, be apparent in reprints thereof.

British Library Cataloguing in Publication Data
A CIP catalogue record for this book
is available from the British Library

Market Structure and Performance
ISBN 978-0-415-26919-3 (hbk)
ISBN 978-0-415-86606-4 (pbk)
Industrial Economics I: 3 Volumes
ISBN 978-0-415-26916-2
Harwood Fundamentals of Pure & Applied Economics
ISBN 978-0-415-26907-0

Market Structure and Performance – The Empirical Research

John S. Cubbin
Queen Mary College, University of London and London Business School

A volume in the Theory of the Firm and Industrial Organization section
edited by

Alexis Jacquemin
Université Catholique de Louvain, Belgium

harwood academic publishers
chur · london · paris · new york · melbourne

Harwood Academic Publishers

Post Office Box 197
London WC2E 9PX
England

58, rue Lhomond
75005 Paris
France

Post Office Box 786
Cooper Station
New York, NY 10276
United States of America

Private Bag 8
Camberwell, Victoria 3124
Australia

Library of Congress Cataloging-in-Publication Data

Cubbin, John.
Market structure and performance: the empirical research/John S. Cubbin; edited by Alexis Jacquemin.
p. cm. -- (Fundamentals of pure and applied economics, ISSN 0191-1708; v. 28. Theory of the firm and industrial organization section)
Bibliography: p.
Includes Index.
1. Industrial organization (Economic theory) I. Jacquemin, Alex. II. Title. III. Series: Fundamentals of pure and applied economics; v. 28. IV. Series: Fundamentals of pure and applied economics. Theory of the firm and industrial organization section.
HD2326.C85 1988
338.6--dc 19 88-20567
CIP

Contents

Introduction to the Series	vii
1. Bain's Methodology	4
2. The Theoretical Background	6
3. Theoretical Concepts Versus Empirical Constructs	26
4. Econometric Problems	42
5. The Determinants of Market Structure	45
6. The Mainstream Tradition – Empirical Results	51
7. Concentration, Wages and Unionization	57
8. Market Structure and Performance – The Key Issues	88
9. The Persistence of Market Power and Profitability	64
10. Summary and Conclusions	65
Acknowledgements	68
Bibliography and References	69
Index	77

Introduction to the Series

Drawing on a personal network, an economist can still relatively easily stay well informed in the narrow field in which he works, but to keep up with the development of economics as a whole is a much more formidable challenge. Economists are confronted with difficulties associated with the rapid development of their discipline. There is a risk of "balkanization" in economics, which may not be favorable to its development.

Fundamentals of Pure and Applied Economics has been created to meet this problem. The discipline of economics has been subdivided into sections (listed inside). These sections include short books, each surveying the state of the art in a given area.

Each book starts with the basic elements and goes as far as the most advanced results. Each should be useful to professors needing material for lectures, to graduate students looking for a global view of a particular subject, to professional economists wishing to keep up with the development of their science, and to researchers seeking convenient information on questions that incidentally appear in their work.

Each book is thus a presentation of the state of the art in a particular field rather than a step-by-step analysis of the development of the literature. Each is a high-level presentation but accessible to anyone with a solid background in economics, whether engaged in business, government, international organizations, teaching, or research in related fields.

Three aspects of *Fundamentals of Pure and Applied Economics* should be emphasized:

— First, the project covers the whole field of economics, not only theoretical or mathematical economics.

— Second, the project is open-ended and the number of books is not predetermined. If new interesting areas appear, they will generate additional books.
— Last, all the books making up each section will later be grouped to constitute one or several volumes of an Encyclopedia of Economics.

The editors of the sections are outstanding economists who have selected as authors for the series some of the finest specialists in the world.

J. Lesourne *H. Sonnenschein*

Market Structure and Performance – The Empirical Research

J.S. CUBBIN

Queen Mary College, University of London and London Business School

Traditionally much economic theorising has taken as its starting point the assumption that supply is organised competitively. However, the competitive model is an artificial distinction which produces very few features found in practice. Where the assumption of competition has been obviously inappropriate the alternative choice for modelling purposes has, until recently, usually been monopoly. This, too, is an artificial abstraction, only recognisable in isolated instances and perhaps this is one reason why there has been a recent resurgence of interest in the theory of oligopoly.

Most industrial markets lie in the grey area between pure competition and monopoly. Products (and services) are typically not homogeneous across firms in an industry and often entry or exit is not costless or instantaneous. Within this grey area "competition" is far removed from the passive behaviour of the purely competitive model. Prices, advertising and promotion, and changes in the products themselves are the means of active competition. It is the results of this kind of competition which determines the range, variety, and prices of goods offered for sale in the modern world.

Apart from the purely positive interest in the mechanics of industrial markets, much academic effort has been motivated by normative considerations. On the one side has been a suspicion that activities regarded by the firms themselves as competitive (such as advertising) are in many instances a means of maintaining monopolistic positions. Within this school of thought the model of pure competition is more than an abstraction; it is regarded as a desirable and more-or-less reasonable policy objective. Against this some economists of a laissez-faire bent claim that the competitive model, especially in its static nature, is an irrelevant benchmark; that monopolies are not in any case sustainable unless supported by the force of law; and those monopolistic elements that exist are the product of government interference and regulation. Acknowledgment of the dynamic and non-price aspects of competition led J.M. Clark [31] to propose a standard of "workable competition" and it is this concept, rather than pure competition, which forms the standard for public policies on competition in industrialised market economies.

Workable competition substitutes oligopolistic rivalry for pure competition. The central question is whether this rivalry is capable of achieving satisfactory levels of performance. Once we move from the static model, however, there are no objective standards of performance for an industry. This led some commentators to define workable competition in terms of structure and conduct. For instance,

> "An industry is workably competitive when (1) there are a considerable number of firms selling closely related products in each market area, (2) these firms are not in collusion, and (3) the long run average cost curve for the new firms is not materially higher than that for the established firm."[1]

Conditions (1) and (2) together ensure both choice for consumers and rivalry amongst sellers to provide the best deal. Condition (3) is Stigler's definition of no entry barriers. Since collusion is generally thought to be more difficult amongst large numbers, a market would be considered workably competitive if there were large numbers of independent suppliers selling similar goods and there were no entry barriers. Competition from outside the market is seen as complementary to internal rivalry. This concept of potential competition is usually attributed to J.B. Clark [30].

> "Let any combination of producers raise the prices beyond a certain limit and it will encounter this difficulty. The new mill that will spring into existence will break down prices; and the fear of these new mills, without their actual coming, is often enough to keep prices from rising to an extortionate height. The mill that has never been built is already a power

[1] J. B. Clark, *The Control of Trusts* (1901)

in the market: for if it will surely be built under certain conditions the effect of this certainty is to keep prices down."

These considerations suggest a number of empirical issues:

1. Is there any connection between the number of competitors and the degree of rivalry?
2. If so, how many competitors are sufficient to produce an outcome so that there is little or no gain from a greater atomization of sellers?
3. What determines the number of sellers?
4. Is the force of potential competition deflected in some industries by entry barriers?
5. Are these entry barriers, if they exist, a necessary concomitant of the technology, a byproduct of rivalry, or consequences of a deliberate strategy of limiting competition?

These kinds of questions are at the core of the Structure-Conduct-Performance (S-C-P) paradigm. "Structure" refers to a description of the industry in terms of the number and size distribution of firms, and any entry barriers arising from the technology of production. "Conduct" (or in some terminology, "behaviour") refers to decisions by firms on pricing, product quality, advertising, product or process development, etc. It encompasses decisions on whether to collude or compete and in which areas of choice. One effect of conduct may be to alter structure in terms of market concentration or entry barriers. The main interest of conduct, however, is that it provides the link from structure to performance.

"Performance" is used in an ambiguous sense. In its most general sense it is an evaluation of the contribution of the industry as a whole to economic welfare. Are costs minimised and prices driven down in line with costs? Has technological advance been satisfactory? Expressed like this it is clear that "performance" is as vague a concept as "workable competition". However, public competition agencies, such as the British Monopolies (and Mergers) Commission, frequently find themselves having to try to answer such difficult questions.

In practical terms performance often boils down to profitability. The essence of the S-C-P paradigm is that differences in structure lead to observable differences in both conduct and performance. In plain words, this means that fewness of sellers and high entry barriers lead to high prices and high profits. The various approaches to testing this deceptively simple proposition are the subject of this study.

The plan of the study is as follows. We devote the next section to a brief description of Bain's pioneering work, which produces an agenda of questions which he left unanswered. Section 2 consists of a brief survey of the theoretical basis of the empirical literature. Section 3 is devoted to problems of the specification and measurement of variables, and section 5 is a brief survey of the econometric problems. Section 6 is devoted to the determinants of market structure. Inevitably, sections 3-7 are concerned with matters of detail and section 8 attempts to put these details into perspective by focussing on the key policy issues.

1. BAIN'S METHODOLOGY

The study which has set the standard for research in this field is Joe S. Bain's *Barriers to New Competition* [6] which was the culmination of work through the 1940s and into the fifties conceived originally under the leadership of E. S. Mason[2] [127]. The time scale of this endeavour reflects the effort put into refining concepts and critically appraising data that was not always present in later empirical research attempting either to build on Bain's contribution or to demolish it.

For example, Bain's original sample contained only 20 industries out of a total list of 452; and this limits the reliability of any general conclusions drawn from the sample, as Bain himself acknowledges. This limited sample size arose from two considerations. The first was the need to choose industries listed in the *Census of Manufacturers* which corresponded to the Chamberlinian notion of a product group. The "industry" may consist of firms producing goods which are not close substitutes since the industry definition may be based on the technology used rather than products produced. Similarly, the "industry" may not contain products which are close substitutes in consumption although not in product (for example plastic and steel buckets).

The second consideration was the great deal of detail that Bain

[2] For a brief history of the field see Shepherd (ch 2) [169].

explored in order to classify his industries. "First, a lengthy preliminary survey was made of each industry, to provide the author with an orientation of its characteristics and a knowledge of the conspicuous blanks in existing information. Second, a detailed set of questions was designed for each industry in turn, to elicit information bearing on the condition of entry therein. Each industry was favoured with a separate and special list of questions, and no general purpose questionnaire was used. The questions generally involved some detailed reference to the specific characteristics of individual industries, and were grouped to refer separately to economies of scale, product differentiation, advantages of established firms, and their absolute cost advantages."

Thus, in the trade-off between numbers of observations and quality of data, Bain chose the latter.

Bain assigned each industry in his sample to one of three categories: substantial; moderate to high; and low barriers to entry. He examined the relationship between high concentration and profitability in each of these categories, and found this to be significant only where barriers to entry were "substantial". The relationship was not continuous; it appeared there was a critical (8-firm) concentration ratio of 70 per cent, implying (in terms of the S-C-P paradigm) a sudden switch in behaviour between collusion and competition. These results appeared consistent with the theoretical framework which suggests that both high concentration and barriers to entry are necessary to maintain a collusive equilibrium.

Bain's work was a major pioneering achievement in the study of industrial organisation. Although he conceded that a sample of 20 industries was too small to draw reliable general conclusions, it was a big improvement on the "one, two or three industries that have constituted the apparent empirical reference of numerous past generalisations in the area under study."

The developments of Bain's work can be viewed as attempts to remedy the two major weaknesses – small sample size and subjectivity. The problem with Bain's technique of evaluation by interview and questionnaire is the element of judgement in assigning industries to entry barrier categories. There may be a subconscious tendency to assign to the "substantial" entry barrier category industries which are known (or thought to be) profitable. This is a well known problem in the methodology of science and is dealt with, for example in medical research, by the use of "double blind" trials where neither the experimenter nor the subject knows whether a certain treatment is being applied. Economists have so far made little use of this technique, partly because it is much more difficult to apply in a non-experimental setting.

The problem of subjective categorization can be dealt with by the substitution of objectively–measured numerical data. For instance the economies of scale entry barrier might be measured by a combination of the ratio of minimum efficient scale to industry output and the cost penalty to suboptimal output levels. The use of such "objective" measures obviates the need for lengthy questionnaires and enables the sample size to be increased.

However, it does not eliminate all subjective choices. Probably the most critical are of subjective choice that remains is in sample industry selection; does an officially designated industry correspond to the notion of a Chamberlinian interdependent group? If this criterion is relaxed more industries can be included but there is an increasing tendency to be over or under-inclusive. Variables will be measured with more error and estimates of the effect of concentration will be biased downwards. This subjectivity seems to act very strongly in this area, and there seems to be a close correspondence between researcher's prior policy beliefs and their empirical findings. One of the most difficult tasks in surveying this field is to filter out these subjective elements. Before we can attempt this task it is necessary to consider some of the details of the conceptual framework.

2. THE THEORETICAL BACKGROUND

Although this monograph is concerned largely with the empirical literature some theoretical discussion is necessary for its proper evaluation. For a more detailed exposition of many of the matters dealt with here the interested reader is referred to [35], [188], [161] [183] or indeed the monograph by Fudenberg and Tyrole [78] in this series.

Bain identified two major features of markets as responsible for determining performance within a market – concentration and entry barriers. His theoretical work, however, was much more concerned with the latter than the former and his contributions here are still central to contemporary analysis.

In recent years, however, it has come to be recognised [138], [63] that properly conceived, entry barrier theory is really a branch of oligopoly theory and that it is necessary to model the interdependencies between incumbents and potential entrants.

2.1. Economic performance

Industrial performance is a concept which has largely been left rather vague, but clearly refers in some sense to economic welfare. The assessment of performance almost inevitably requires both a measuring system (or metric) and a base from which to carry out the measurement. The problems of measuring almost any kind of economic welfare are well known and should be taken as implicit qualifiers to the following.

Two alternative bases of measurement suggest themselves. One possibility is the aggregation of producers' and consumers' surplus generated by the industry, and represents an answer to the question "How much worse off would society be if this industry did not exist?" Whilst one might conceive of some sort of answer to this question using partial equilibrium analysis for the video games industry, for example, in general any attempt to do this for such a core industry as automobiles is fraught with difficulties. Even if a credible figure could be arrived at for one industry the task of doing so for a wide range of industries would be a mammoth undertaking, and in any case it is not clear for what purpose such a measure would be useful.

An alternative basis for measurement, and the one used in practice, is the competitive norm. The ultimate motivation for this is the notion of the Pareto optimality of a full competitive equilibrium even though it is widely recognised that for any one industry in a imperfect economy the competitive outcome is unlikely to be the second best standard. However since we do not have the means to calculate this "second best" solution the competitive norm is our best *practicable* basis.

An example of this approach is provided by Dansby and Willig[3] [59] whose proposed indices are for the purpose of directing government intervention into conduct. Their approach is partial equilibrium and marginalist. Specifically, the increment to welfare from producing an

---

[3] See also the papers by Encaoua and Jacquemin [70] and Pindyck [145].

extra unit of output is the gap between price (= consumers' marginal willingness to pay) minues marginal cost (= opportunity cost of marginal resources foregone). Using base prices as scaling factor this immediately suggest the Lerner Index $\sum(P_i - MC_i)/P_i$ as the "performance gradient index" for firm i. This leaves the problem of aggregating across firms. Weighting firm output adjustment by the unit price of each firm leads to the "industry performance gradient"

$$\varnothing = [\sum((P_i - MC_i)/P_i)^2]^{1/2}$$

which is one way of generalising the Lerner index to multiple-firm industries. Furthermore $\varnothing$ will, in certain circumstances, be closely related to measure of concentration, depending upon the type of conduct characterising the industry. For example, in a Cournot industry $\varnothing = 1/\eta\sqrt{H}$ where η is the industry demand elasticity and H is the Herfindahl index of concentration, whereas in an industry with n firms maximising joint profits with a fringe of competitive firms then

$$\varnothing = (\sqrt{n}/\eta)CR_n$$

where n is the n-firm concentration ratio.

The underlying presumption behind these indices is that, at least in the first instance, correction of misallocation is best carried out by expanding the outputs of existing firms. However, Figure 1 shows an example where the Dansby and Willig measure fails to indicate the need for industry expansion.

Let the industry price be P_1 initially and output of a representative firm be q_1. Welfare is improved by an expansion of output to q_2 which will lead to a fall in price to P_2. Industry output should still be expanded, although not by the expansion of existing firms, but rather by the entry of new firms. This is measured by P_2–AC_2, the price – *average* cost margin, and under the assumption of produce homogeneity this is measurable by the rate of return[4].

In summary, there are two margins at which output can be expanded, the intra-firm and the inter-firm, and as a rule of thumb we can say that Lerner-type indices measure the former and rates of

[4] Where products are differentiated it has yet to be convincingly demonstrated that a free entry equilibrium generates the greatest welfare. See [99] for a discussion of this point.

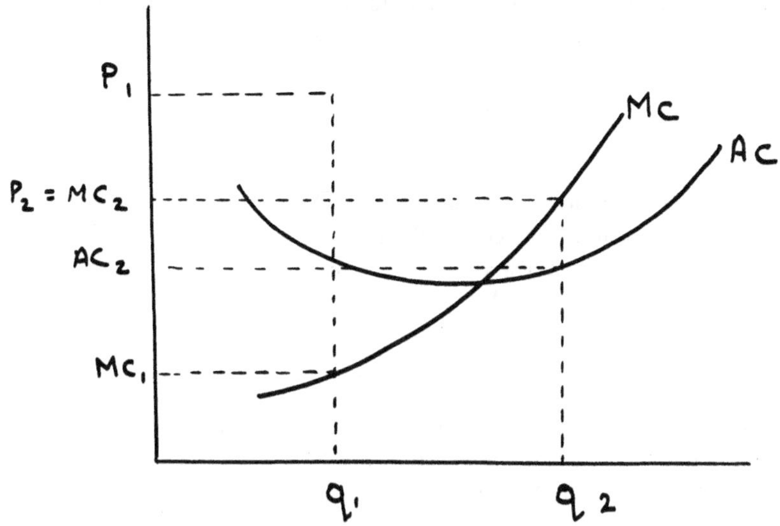

return the latter. Furthermore, as we discuss below the former are proximately determined by the degree of collusion whereas the latter are more closely related to the height of entry barriers, and these are discussed in turn in the following sections.

2.2. Oligopoly theory and the effects of concentration

Within oligopoly theory, the Cournot [44] model still holds sway as a standard of comparison. Its appeal is fourfold: i) by assuming quantity-setting behaviour and homogenous products it facilitates comparison with monopoly and perfectly competitive outcomes; ii) the solution has the game-theoretic property of a Nash equilibrium; iii) it predicts a continuous monotonic relationship between concentration and the deviation from the competitive outcome, with the latter as the limiting case for large numbers, and the standard monopoly result emerging when there is only one firm; iv) it dictates the use of a particular concentration measure, thus apparently eliminating a major problem for the empirical researcher. The paper which was most influential in gaining recognition for these merits is by Cowling and Waterson, whose conclusions may be summarised as follows.

Given an N firm homogeneous oligopoly, where firms have different cost functions, the Cournot oligopoly outcome is one in which

$$\frac{\sum(P-MC_i)s_i}{P} = \frac{H}{\eta} \tag{1}$$

Where P = "industry" price
MC_i = marginal cost of the ith firm
s_i = Market share of the ith firm
η = industry elasticity of demand
H = Herfindahl–Hirschman index of market concentration = $\sum^{n}{}_{i}s^{2}{}_{i}$

If one then makes the further assumption that each firm operates in a region of constant returns to scale that MC_i = average cost of firm i then equation (1) can be rewritten as

$$\frac{\pi}{R} = \frac{H}{\eta} \tag{2}$$

where π and R are the industry aggregate (economic) profits and revenue. The acid test of such a model – derived explicitly for empirical purposes – is its empirical support, which we shall be examining later. However, the Cowling and Waterson paper was widely adopted as powerful expression of the structure performance paradigm, having the considerable virtues of both elegance and precision.

Equation (2) shows an apparently fundamental strutural relationship between concentration and profits where "behaviour" or "the solution concept" is held constant. Cowling and Waterson also amended their fundamental equation to allow for systematic variations in behaviour with concentration using the concept of conjectural variations. To be specific consider a firm's profit function

$$\pi_i = p(q_i + \Sigma q_j) - c(q_i) \tag{3}$$

The first order condition for a maximum is

$$\frac{\vartheta \pi_i}{\vartheta q_i} = (1 + \sum_{j \neq i} \frac{dq_j}{dq_i})p - c \qquad (4)$$

Writing $\lambda = \Sigma \frac{dq_j}{dq_i}$ and aggregating as for as the Cournot model

lead to the following

$$\frac{\pi}{R} = \frac{H(1 + \lambda)}{\eta} \qquad (5)$$

This logical extension to the Cournot model is usually justified on the grounds that one should expect that collusion becomes easier with increasing concentration. At this point the model loses its precision. One may postulate, for example, that $(1 + \lambda) = H^{\propto}$ so that

$$\frac{\pi}{R} = \frac{H^{(1 + \propto)}}{\eta} \qquad (6)$$

and, taking logs, can derive the straightforward linear estimating equation.

$$\log(\frac{\pi}{R}) = (1 + \propto)\log H - \log \eta \qquad (7)$$

Since $\propto$ is positive the coefficient on log H in this equation should therefore be greater than 1.

Not that the functional form is no longer purely derived from theoretical considerations – the term $H^{\propto}$ is essentially *ad hoc*. Of course, there are always *ad hoc* decision to be made when undertaking empirical work and this one seems as defensible as many. However, the issue of the degree of collusion, its relationship to conjectural variations, and the possible link with concentration is fundamental to the SCP paradigm, particularly in relation to policy considerations.

Conjectural variations versus collusion: consistent conjectures

Equations (3) and (4) above are those of a follower. In the Cournot model the firm accepts other firm's outputs as given; under conjectural variations it accepts their *reactions* as given. Under neither model are reactions given explicitly, only implicitly as a consequence of their equilibrium behaviour. It is a well-known property of the Cournot model that the reactions that one would derive from the Cournot model would, if treated seriously, produce non zero conjectural variations. If we adopt the equilibrium conditions of the Cournot model as the basis of its *disequilibrium* behaviour, the model is inconsistent. Whilst this causes little concern to game theorists who avoid the extensive form, it has been a worry to other economists. One recent attempt to deal with this apparent inconsistency, influenced partly by the rational expectations revolution in macroeconomics, has been to analyze models of consistent conjectures [16], [15] and [106]. These are conjectural variations models with the added condition that the equilibrium conditions produce behaviour in the neighbourhood of the equilibrium such that conjectures will be shown to be true.

At first blush this would seem to solve two problems in one – namely the inconsistency problem and the problem of where the conjectures come from. These hopes were disappointed, however, since under one definition the only consistent equilibrium turned out to be the competitive equilibrium (and thus was inconsistent with the S.C.P. paradigm) or, under a broader definition, almost any equilibrium could be defined to be consistent, [15] and [106].

This episode was, however, fruitful in reawakening interest in oligopoly amongst theorists. Since these recent contributions have yet to make their mark on empirical work, the reader is referred to the volume by Fudenberg and Tyrole [78] in this series for further details. However, one relevant point is that these recent theoretical developments have been concerned with the oligopoly "game" – (and, incidentally other games such as the macroeconomic policy "game" – as a process. The consistency problem is one of consistency over time and the ability of players to make threats that are credible.

Threats, conjectures and collusion

Conjectural variations have been widely used as a way of modelling the degree of collusion, and the Cowling and Waterson article is now probably the most widely cited theoretical basis for empirical work. As the above discussion makes clear, there are severe problems if conjectured variations represent the equilibrium or steady-state behaviour of the other oligopolists (or rather comparative-static type changes therein). On the other hand, model consistency requires that conjectures are derived from a coherent view of rivals' strategy.

The notion of a strategy is wider than that of an equilibrium behaviour, in that it specifies behaviour in all feasible situations. Models of conjectural variations imply very simple strategies of the form "follow rivals' output changes by a fixed proportional amount." As far as this author is aware, no rationale for this kind of strategy has yet been produced.

The closest to a rationalisation of something like such a strategy comes from work on experimental games. A strategy, however complicated, should in principle be capable of being written down as a computer program describing the next move in terms of the current situation, other players' last moves, or even the whole history of the game. Axelrod [2] set up a repeated 2-person 2×2 game with a Prisoners' Dilemma payoff matrix structure and invited game theorists from many disciplines to submit FORTRAN computer programs to enter a tournament, where each program "played" every other program. He found that the winning programs were those with strategies that produced co-operative behaviour on both sides. Over one hundred strategies were submitted, many of them involving complex rules designed to default optimally on any co-operative "equilibrium reached". The winning strategy was in fact very simple and consisted of co-operation for the first move and every move immediately following one on which the opponent co-operated. If the opponent defaulted in an attempt to exploit the apparent co-operation of this strategy, the program produced one unco-operative response, followed by a continuation of co-operation. Hence the name of this strategy – "TIT FOR TAT". Although this program did not necessarily "win" individual games it managed to win the tournament by inducing a high proportion co-operative outcomes.

The positive contribution of this work to oligopoly theory is to show how a collusive solution can be maintained. More importantly it demonstrates the distinction between equilibrium (collusive) and disequilibrium (punishing defection) behaviour. The disequilibrium behaviour is short lived. Furthermore, with two players both following this strategy this disequilibrium behaviour would never be observed since there would be a permanent collusive equilibrium. Bilateral TIT FOR TAT is therefore observationally equivalent to simple collusion. This illustrates the general point that the disequilibrium behaviour cannot be deduced from observing the equilibrium.

The oligopoly equivalent of TIT FOR TAT is a punishment of deviations from the collusive solution by matching output (or price, in a price-setting model) exactly. Partial matching fails to achieve the fully collusive solution and will therefore be suboptimal. Therefore the only conjectural variations which Axelrod's results seem to justify are unitary ones, whether of the price or output variety. This is the approach taken by the present author [48], [50] and p. 36 below) in a development of Stigler's model which shows how variations in the ability to detect and immediately punish non collusive behaviour result in a set of equilibria which are analogous to conjectural variations equilibria, but which differ fundamentally in their disequilibrium behaviour.

An analytical paper in the spirit of Axelrod (but inspired by Stigler [173]) is that by Green and Porter [88], who consider an n-firm quantity setting cartel facing noise demand. The cartel's policy is to set a collusive level of output, a trigger price (below which output is expanded to the Cournot level in punishment mode), and an optimal punishment length. The degree to which the quantity produced approaches the monopoly level is then a function of the noise on the demand side. The model is therefore useful in drawing attention to the role of information in oligopoly.

We started this section with the Cournot model and its conjectural variations extension, noting a central property of such models to be a strong relationship between concentration and price-cost margins. Suppose that one finds sparce empirical evidence of such a relationship, what conclusions should be drawn? Either the empirical evidence is wrong, or the Cournot/conjectural variations models are inadequate descriptions of reality. Fortunately, there are alternative oligopoly models. However, these alternatives seem to have in common the property that they can best be described in terms of pricing behaviour, rather than quantity setting. The first major rival to Cournot's model was that of Bertrand, who pointed out that ostensibly the same (Nash equilibrium) behaviour, but in the context of price setting, leads to a competitive equilibrium. From this, two conclusions follow. i) Only two firms are necessary to ensure competitive behaviour, and ii) with a given solution concept it may matter considerably whether one characterises oligopoly as price- or quantity-setting. The majority of economists seem to have been reluctant to accept these implications, and when Edgeworth pointed out that, given certain capacity limitations, disequilibrium behaviour produces price oscillations, this was enough to relegate the Bertrand model to the footnotes of oligopoly theory.

In recent years, however, a more sophisticated version of the Bertrand model, in the form of the notion of contestable markets [8], [4] has enjoyed considerable discussion. Consideration of disequilibrium dynamics is avoided in this model since only one of the duopolists need to be in actual production; the other exists merely to threaten entry. The model requires capital to be mobile in both directions across markets. For this reason the leading examples of contestable markets are in the transportation industry (inter-city airlines, interstate trucking), since this guarantees physical mobility from one market area to another. From the contestable markets literature we learn that even monopolies cannot operate monopolistically if entry barriers are low enough. W. G. Shepherd has argued that this fact was well appreciated before the contestable markets uprising, and that it therefore offers us little or no new insight.

What it may have achieved, however, is to reinstate price setting behaviour as worthy of consideration within oligopoly theory. It is generally assumed that, since quantity setting results in a price and vice versa, there is no fundamental objection to analysing pricing behaviour "as if" firms were quantity setting. However, we have already referred to the Bertrand model which, using the same solution concept produces a radically different outcome. The same applies to all standard conjectural variations models (except with the joint monopoly outcome.) Similarly, Kamien and Schwartz [106] have shown that the equivalent definitions of consistent conjectures produce different outcomes under pricing and quantity setting behaviour. So the difference between quantity and price setting is not trivial. For further discussion see [55].

In general, and allowing for product differentiation, price setting behaviour leads to lower prices and greater quantities than quantity setting behaviour. This is essentially because the effective elasticity of demand is higher in the price setting case. See, for example [29].

One possible reason for many economists' reluctance to deal with price-setting oligopoly may be the mathematical difficulty that arises with the existence of two prices in the homogeneous products case. The obvious answer to this is to acknowledge that many oligopolies produce differentiated products. This is already done in an *ad hoc* way by the introduction of advertising intensity into structure performance models, but the formal analyis of product differentiation in oligopoly is still in its infancy, more than fifty years after the publication of E. H. Chamberlin's *Theory of Monopolistic Competition* [27] and Joan Robinson's *The Economics of Imperfect Competition* [154]. This is not the place to ponder on the apparent failure of the "product differentiation" revolution. Philosophical problems in defining the exact boundaries of the market may have played a part, as may an over emphasis on the so-called "excess capacity" theorem in the early days. For whatever reason, a resurgence of interest only came about after Lancaster showed how differentiated products could be modeled as a package of homogeneous characteristics. For a modern review of the theory of product differentiation see Ireland [99].

One of the few major economists who maintained an interest in pricing by companies (rather than the fictional auctioneer) was G. J. Stigler. His many well-known contributions include research into pricing behaviour [175] which appears to cast considerable doubt on the kinked demand curve hypothesis as a general description of oligopoly behaviour. However his model of oligopoly is perhaps less well-known than it ought to be, and has the following to recommend it:-

1. It is explicitly a model of pricing behaviour, not quantity setting.
2. Conjectured behaviour is based upon profit maximising principles.
3. Equilibrium and disequilibrium behaviour are distinguished.

The profit maximising principles are those captured by the Prisoners' Dilemma game. Oligopolists have a collective incentive to collude, and an individual incentive to undermine the collusive solution. The equilibrium is the resolution of these two opposing forces. The present author [50] has shown how the position of this equilibrium between the joint monopoly and Nash equilibria depends on the speed and certainty of retaliation against price-cutting behaviour.

The resultant formula for the price-cost margin is

$$\frac{P_i - MC_i}{P_i} = \frac{1}{\propto \eta^I + (1-\propto)\eta_i^f} \tag{8}$$

where η^I = aggregate industry demand elasticity.
η_i^f = firm i's own price elasticity for a unilateral price change.
$\propto$ = degree of apparent collusion.

which may be interpreted in terms of the probability of detection and retaliation, the delay in retaliation, or the probabilistic rate of retaliation. In the Stigler model this retaliation needs only to be threatened in order to induce conformity with the stable equilibrium. Insofar as the threat is insufficient and (but) oligopolists actually carry our such retaliatory measures the Stigler model may perhaps be said to anticipate the discovery of TIT FOR TAT (see p. 13 above) as a successful strategy for inducing co-operation.

One interesting aspect of Stigler's paper is that, although the number of sellers (and therefore seller concentration) has an effect in the expected direction of the ease of collusion, the model is much richer than, for example, the Cournot model, in the list of influences on the price-cost margin. These include not only the number of sellers, but the number of buyers and the probability of repeat purchase. To these may be added the size and frequency of orders and the availability of information on competitors' sales. The consequence of the greater number of variables, many of them uncorrelated with seller concentration, is that the relationship between concentration and profitability is greatly attenuated. Thus, although there may be successful collusion (perhaps implicit rather than explicit) this is determined by several factors and is not necessarily restricted to the most concentrated industries. Indeed, collusion may for one reason or another be very difficult to sustain amongst several of the latter. Amongst these reasons may of course be the threat of antitrust action. Another factor may be the tendency in some markets (concentrated and otherwise) for price collusion to foster non-price competition which undermines margins. It is sometimes claimed that the medical (and in some countries legal) professions are amongst the most successfully collusive industries. These are unconcentrated, which perhaps gives them an air of innocence and allows them to avoid, even to justify publicly the avoidance of, both price and non-price competition.

What these theoretical models of oligopoly have in common is that their prediction are in terms of the Lerner index, or price cost margin. Some authors have taken this to mean that this is the appropriate theoretical dependent variable for empirical work on the effects of concentration. Alternative definitions of the dependent variables are discussed further below, but note that the issue is not as clear cut as the discussion of oligopoly theory indicates. For existing firms, competition is very much about decisions affecting incremental output, and the Lerner index is an appropriate measure for such decisions, as we saw in our discussion of industry performance gradients above.

For potential entrants, however, whether to become a competitor depends on the prospective increase in wealth for an incremental capital investment decision. The test for such decisions can, subject to the usual reservations, be expressed as whether the rate of return on that investment exceeds the opportunity cost of funds. Within Bain's definition, discussed below, the test of whether an entry barrier exists is the presence of supernormal profits without inducing entry. Price-marginal cost margins are only relevant insofar as they have a bearing on price-average cost margins. To be sure, long run marginal and average costs are equal under constant returns to scale, and so are the short run concepts as long as there is no excess capacity. However, all the assumptions necessary to justify particular definitions of the dependent variable are rarely discussed in the empirical literature. In practice the true Lerner index is scarcely ever used, but an "approximation" based on average, rather than marginal cost.

By definition the relationship between the price-marginal cost margin and the price-average cost margin is

$$\frac{P - ATC}{P} = \frac{P - AVC}{P} - \frac{FC}{R} \tag{9}$$

where ATC = average total cost
AVC = average variable cost
FC = fixed cost
R = revenue

and if we assume that variable and marginal cost are equal then

$$\frac{P - MC}{P} = \frac{P - AVC}{P} \quad (10)$$

$$\frac{P - ATC}{P} = \frac{P - MC}{P} - \frac{FC}{R} \quad (11)$$

Thus, depending on assumptions about the relationship between FC/R and capital intensity and the constancy of marginal and variable cost, the two measures may be related to each other, provided variations in capital intensity are allowed for. Furthermore one may wish to justify the use of (P - AVC)/P *either* as a measure of the Lerner index or as measure of (P - ATC)/P. In the latter case the fixed cost element must be allowed for by including K/R as an additional explanatory variable.

2.3 Barriers to entry

"When I use a word" said Humpty Dumpty in a rather scornful tone "it means just what I choose it to mean—neither more nor less" [22]. The difficulties caused by non standard definitions (equilibrium/disequilibrium, static/dynamic) will be familiar to economists in many specialisations, but nowhere has the unwillingness to stick to a standard definition caused more confusion than in the question of entry barriers. As an extreme example, students when they first meet the concept are apt to argue that keeping price low in order to deter entry is a form of entry barrier. Thus, a contestable market, or one in competitive equilibrium, must have a very high entry barrier as it is not worth entering, or so the argument goes. Needless to say, such an interpretation of entry barriers does not take us very far in understanding industrial organisation. Yet any empirical analysis based purely on rates of entry into a market is liable to suffer from the same paradox. Von Weizsacher [189] has proposed a definition of entry barriers in terms the existence or otherwise of a welfare loss. The objections to this are, firstly, that welfare loss is notoriously difficult to measure conclusively, and secondly, it creates problems for the methodological distinction between positive and normative propositions in economics. If all entry barriers are bad, what do we call "entry barriers" that may be desirable? To take an extreme example, most people would probably agree that legal barriers to entering the nuclear explosive industry are desirable. Are we to count the loss of consumer surplus to the potential customers of such an industry (including terrorists and maniacs) the basis for calling such a barrier a barrier? Stigler's definition is more acceptable, but still raises problems:

> "A barrier to entry may be defined as a cost of producing (at some or every rate of output) which must be borne by a firm which seeks to enter an industry but which is not borne by firms already in the industry." [175] (p. 67).

There are two objections to this, one fairly trivial and the other one more substantive. The more trivial problem is the concentration on *cost* advantages, which restricts the usefulness of the definition to industries producing homogeneous products. One might surmount this problem by specifying the cost of producing a given quality, or even a product with identical demand characteristics, were it not for the more fundamental problem that it ignores possible advantages from being the first mover. (See [160]) for the classic account of the way these work or, more recently, [64]. Briefly, the argument is that incumbents, by making investments with a low value in alternative uses (such as market-specific plant, or advertising) engage in a credible commitment to the industry which, paradoxically, gives them an advantage in the bargaining game. (By way of analogy, Schelling notes that Caesar, by crossing the Rubicon with his army and then burning his boats behind him made such a credible commitment to fighting to the last man that bloodless victory was assured.) The appealing thing about Stigler's definition is the notion of fair play and equal rights for all producers. Unfortunately these are normative concepts and should therefore be analysed separately from the essentially positive notion of entry barriers attributable to Bain. Bain's definition of the height of the entry barrier facing a potential entrant is the margin by which established firms can raise their price above the competitive price level persistently without attracting entry.

He identified four possible sources of entry—cost advantages, scale economies, "product differentiation" advantages, and absolute capital requirements. Salop [158] has suggested a further categorisation of entry barriers into natural and strategic types—The former are a function of technology and/or historical accident. Strategic entry barriers are any created deliberately by incumbents. A favourite example of this is the holding of excess capacity [170], [64] and [162].

The distinction may be important when it comes to an evaluation of a company's competitive behaviour by competitive policy agencies. Natural advantages would not normally be considered culpable whereas strategically erected barriers might be the focus of antitrust attention. Thus the distinction between strategic and natural entry barriers acknowledge entry barriers as a concept in positive economics, and introduces a separate classification with normative content.

This distinction between normative and positive concepts of entry barriers is illustrated by the absolute cost advantage category. Clearly such an advantage can explain persistently high profits without inducing entry. However the source of such a cost advantage, if it is traded in a competitive market, would normally expect to earn a factor rent, and if that source also happens to be the beneficiary of the supernormal profit, no misallocation has occurred. The factor rent appears as a monopoly profit. A similar argument can be put on the "product differentiation" advantage side: if the demand advantage arises from the wisdom of the profit beneficiaries in hiring designers or in setting up an organisational structure in such a way that superior products are produced, the "supernormal profits" are merely factor rents to superior entrepreneurial ability. Nonetheless, the positive economic analysis still holds; there is an observed supernormal return on invested capital which is explained by the entry barrier of demand advantage. The normative analysis is a second stage.

To illustrate this, consider the well-worn example of New York cab drivers and their expensive medallions, which give them the right to operate charging (presumably) above competitive prices. A non-pioneering cab driver entering this market only earns a normal return on his medallion investment. The original cab-driving instigators of the entry-limiting legislation earned a factor rent on their ability to influence politicians, capitalised into the value of medallions. A welfare analysis of this entry barrier would probably suggest that (in the absence of externalities, etc.) this rent was unwarranted, and that the entry barrier represents a distortion. This example incidentally has implications for the way rates of return should be measured. "Capital investment" should exclude items which are essentially entry fees.

In practice, cost advantages turn out to play only a minor role in the determination of empirical entry barriers. One reason may be that such advantages are difficult to measure systematically across the number of industries necessary for statistical analysis. More to the point, careful case study approaches of the Bain type tend to come up with a few isolated examples.

One major qualification to this statement is in order, however. If we are to believe the arguments of the Boston Consulting Group (BCG), there is a mechanism producing systematic cost advantages for incumbent firms. This is the so-called "experience" effect and is based on an apparent observed regularity in industrial markets. This regularity may be stated as follows: every time cumulative output of a product is doubled the real price of the product falls to X% of its previous level. X is typically 70 or 80. Thus we may observe 70 or 80 per cent experience curves by plotting log price on the vertical axis and log (cumulative output) on the horizontal axis. From this BCG, at least in their earlier work, conclude that costs of production follow a similar course.

There have been a number of criticisms of the BCG approach. First, BCG tend to report their results by drawing thick lines on diagrams, where neither the number of observations nor the goodness of fit are quite as strong as one might expect from a "law of nature". Secondly, what effect there is seems to be a hotch-potch of several effects, only some of which are cost based. For example, there may be a learning effect for manual operatives, but laboratory studies show a much more limited effect, in terms of both size and duration, than that claimed by BCG. There is undoubtedly also some learning on the job by plant engineers, fine tuning of the plant, and endogenous technical progress at work, all of which may give short term advantages to incumbents.

However, some at least of the experience curve effect is also due to pricing behaviour. "Skim-the-cream" pricing is a form of price discrimination using time as the market separation mechanism. High-valuation users of the product may be willing to pay a high price to get the product in the early stages of its life cycle; low-valuation users have to wait until later. This pricing strategy also has entry-deterrent properties. The expectation of a steady decline acts to deter entrants who spot short run profitable opportunities, but fear that costs will never be recovered. Finally, the price behaviour may be an apparent artefact of management accounting procedures. The author has been told on more than one occasion by firms that they were able to undercut their competitors' prices because previous accumulated volumes meant that development and tooling costs had been written off.

(This rationalisation may seem strange to economists, but if it gives a good approximation to optimal policy it will have survival value).

The experience curve has been used in a number of ways by BCG. Principally it seems to be a paradigm around which data can be organised. Some firms have found it useful as a basis for setting targets for plant management. In terms of corporate strategy, however, the main advice proffered by BCG seems to have been to maximise market share. Responding to the critism that, without considering the costs of market share expansion, this could be a self-destructive strategy, BCG seem to have modified their advice in this respect in recent years.

However, there is an implication that market share, apart from being the means by which cumulative output is increased and costs lowered, is an indication of cumulative output and hence of cost advantage. Since a high market share takes time to build up, it is probably reasonable to infer in the majority of cases a close relationship between market share and cumulative output and hence cost advantage arising from the experience effect outlined above. Furthermore, this cost advantage is probably necessary to keep a high market share as a viable equilibrium position.

This discussion has taken us into the realms of causation, dynamics, and the importance of market share. These are dealt with further below. Before these can be discussed properly the static arguments concerning entry barriers and scale economies must be reviewed.

The theoretical basis of scale economies as an entry barrier involves three elements: the definition of entry barriers, price versus quantity setting, and first-mover advantages.

The need for a positive, rather than a normative definition of entry barriers in order to keep the issues clear is made clear by a careful reading of Stigler's article. Stigler's [174] definition of an entry barrier as a cost bourne by the entrant but not the incumbent seems to be based on a notion of fairness rather than an attempt to explain supernormal profit. By this standard, as long as the same technology is available to entrants as incumbents no entry barrier is said to exist.

However, as a number of authors have shown, if entrants take incumbents' output as given (the so-called Sylos postulate) they must assume that the effect of their entry will be to depress industry prices. (Paradoxically, and somewhat confusingly, this effect is reduced if the entrant's product is differentiated to the extent of being able to find its own market niche).

The contestable markets hypothesis (Baumol et al. [8]) turns the Sylos postulate on its head. One of the key assumptions is that *price* will be unaltered following entry. In quantity space, this implies the incumbents in the short-run accepting large declines in sales, and is probably no more realistic than the Sylos postulate. The major contribution of the contestable markets analysis is the elucidation of the fact that the traditional combination of scale economies and a steep market demand curve is not sufficient to produce an entry barrier effect.

2.4 Considerations outside standard oligopoly theory

1. *Strategic groups*

One of the problems of applying pure oligopoly theory is that, for purposes of practical model building, many potentially important aspects of reality are ignored. Oligopolistic behaviour takes place in a historical context and existing firms find themselves in a market for different reasons and equipped with different perceptions of the market. A good example of this is found in Newman's [136] concept of strategic groups. Compare a firm with production capacity in industry X but whose main business is in a related industry Y (perhaps Y is downstream of X). This firms interest in X will be mainly to ensure that what happens in X will not disrupt industry Y and will be willing to sacrifice profits in X in order to ensure this. By contrast a firm whose whose entire business is X will be more committed to the profitability of that industry. The two types of firms will follow different strategies and may be considered as belonging to different *strategic groups*. Lack of goal congruence and communication difficulties arising from different perceptions will undermine the potential for cooperative behaviour. Newman supports this argument by empirical work which shows a much less significant relationship of price-cost margins will concentration amongst strategically heterogeneous groups.

2. *Strategy structure, and intra-industry variation*

Strategies involving diversification not only bring added complexity into oligopolistic interactions, they also create organizational problems for the firms involved. In his famous study of four Du Pont, General Motors, Sears and Standard Oil of New Jersey, Chandler [28] showed how different types of diversifying expansion led ultimately to the adoption of the multi-divisional (M-) form of operation and the hypothesis that corporate structure follows strategy has shown to be fairly well supported in European countries also. Armour and Teece [1] tested the relative efficiency of the M-form structure for a sample of petroleum firms and found that for the period 1956-68 adoption of the M-form was associated with a two percentile point rise in productivity. By 1969-73, however, when the M-form was widely diffused (and presumably most companies were close to their optimal structure) there was no observable effect. The superiority of the M-form for diversified enterprises was independently confirmed by Cable [20] for the UK. Williamson's [191] work provides a comprehensive theoretical framework for the analysis of corporate structure. One of the principle advantages of the M-form structure is that it creates an "internal capital market" where the costs of monitoring and control are less than in the external market. Because of their different traditions and legal systems other countries have evolved organisational forms that achieve some of the same ends. For example Encoua and Jacquemin [71] examine the case of French Industrial Groups and Goto [85] discusses the major types of Japanese business groupings.

3. *Ownership and control*

The need for the multi-divisional form can be seen as an example of principle agent problems and a number of studies have examined the relationship between profitability, growth, and the extent to which ownership is dispersed. Many of these studies are listed in [54]. A full specification would require the inclusion of market power variables in addition to variables representing control type (since in a competitive industry there would be no room for the exercise of managerial discretion of the emergence of X inefficiency). However, only a minority of such studies (e.g. [140] and [96]) specifically take this aspect into account, and as may be expected the improved specification produces results consistent with the managerialist hypothesis. A fairly general finding in this literature is a positive correlation between owner control on the one hand and profitability and high growth rate on the other. Grabowski and Mueller [87] have suggested that the position of a company in its life cycle is an intervening variable. Young quoted companies, they argue, tend to be not owner controlled and fast growing, and also, arguably, profitable.

4. Other firm-specific factors

Our discussion of strategic groups, corporate structure, and the effect of the separation of ownership from control should make it apparent that industries are much more complex than the text book ideal of N identical firms. Motivations, perceptions and organisational flexibility are all potential sources of both inter- and intra-industry variations in performance. If we add to this company-specific factors such as location advantages, product differentiation and particular random factor endowments (especially management) we should expect to observe a substantial degree of intra-industry variation in performance, overlaying any industry effects. Thus, whatever the merits of the structure-conduct-performance paradigm it would be unrealistic to expect it to explain all the observed variation in company performance. Although we have outlined some effects here, the theory of intra-industry performance variations is relatively underdeveloped.

3. THEORETICAL CONCEPTS VERSUS EMPIRICAL CONSTRUCTS

As long as one sticks to pure theory the definition of, say, an industry can be fairly straightforward—the set of firms producing a homogeneous product. To test any theory empirically, however, one needs to translate concepts into operational measures which take into account certain features of the real world, such as the fact that products are not homogeneous and that firms typically produce several products. In this section we consider the problem of the choice of empirical measures for theoretical concepts.

3.1 Industry and firm

The structure-performance paradigm draws upon oligopoly theory, which is concerned with groups of firms whose actions are interdependent. This group is normally divided into two sets: those already producing and potential producers (entrants). The latter is generally unobservable. Setting aside this problem an ideal industry is, therefore, a set of producers whose actions can be considered interdependent. This is most obviously the case where firms are producing reasonably close substitutes, and hence are competitors. To find the competitors of any one firm one asks the question "If I lower (raise) my price, whose sales will suffer (gain) the most?" or conversely "whose price-lowering (increasing) strategies would lower (raise) my sales most?" In markets where transport costs are not significant these questions will frequently yield a closed group of firms all competing with each other. Where transport costs are important, however, the "competitor" relation may not be transitive (A competes with B who competes with C but A and C do not compete) and this gives rise to further problems of defining industrial concentration, to which we shall return below. Even in the absence of transport costs, however, the boundaries between markets may not be hard-and-fast. This becomes most apparent in antitrust policy cases; defending firms typically seek to claim that they are really less concentrated and face more competition than is alleged by the prosecuting authorities. Over the years there have been arguments concerning "Cellophane" and other wrapping materials; copper and aluminium insulated electrical cables; metal cans and glass containers; and several others.

This might suggest some arbitrary cross-elasticity cut-off point. However, even if this could be measured satisfactorily it would be of no use since it is not a technological feature, but depends on firms' behaviour[5]. At high prices substitutes are more easily found than at low prices (and recall that (entry-blockaded) monopolists operate in the elastic part of their demand curve).

---

[5] See R. Posner, *Antitrust Law: An Economic Perspective;* Chicago 1976, pp. 125–134.

Even if a technological measure of demand-substitutability could be measured (say, at the "competitive" price levels) supply-side substitutability can be important in determining the list of each firm's competitors. There is supply-side substitutability where, without incurring any insignificant extra costs, firms may switch their production to products which are good substitutes on the demand side. One may think of this as a way of allowing for the most obvious potential entrants, and is most likely to occur where firms are using very similar technologies.

Official definitions of industries (as in the U.S. Census or the U.K. Census of Production) tend to be dominated by supply-side substitutability—or, at least, to group enterprises according to similarity of production processes using the same raw materials. The classification therefore typically refers to activities rather than commodities. Since new markets probably probably turn over faster than new processes or materials this makes the classification easier to produce and with more continuity, even if this is often at the expense of "ideal" definitions according to the structure-performance paradigm. Different countries base their classification systems to a different degree on the United Nations "International Standard Industrial Classification" (ISIC). To give one example, in some countries the man-made fibres industry is included in the textiles industry, in others it is classified under the chemical industry. The countries of the EEC are, however, moving closer to a common system of classification (NACE[6]).

Data pertaining to standard industries are generally collected at the plant or establishment level, which is defined as the smallest unit which can provide the information normally required for an economist census. Even at this level more than one activity is carried out at one address and where it is not possible to obtain separate figures for each activity the aggregate figures are assigned to the most important one. Figures from these establishement returns can then be aggregated.

To take an example, the NACE system is fairly typical in being arranged on the decimal system:

[6] EUROSTAT, statistical office of the European Communities. General Industrial Classification of Economic Activities within the European Communities.

Level of aggregation	Name of unit	NACE number	Name
1 digit	division	4	Other manufacturing industries
2 digit	class	41	Food, drink and tobacco
3 digit	group	413	Manufacture of dairy products
4 digit	Sub-group	413.1	Processing of milk: butter and cheesemaking
5 digit	item	413.12	Buttermaking

Where the decimal system is used the number of digits is the least ambiguous way of referring to the level of aggregation employed. In particular the terms "group" and "sub-group" mean different aggregation levels in different circumstances. It is generally the case that data availability is better the greater the degree of aggregation whereas markets generally conform better to finer levels of aggregation. In most cases the 3 digit level seems to be appropriate to capture substitution on the supply side, but in general the 4 or even 5 digit level looks more appropriate to capture demand substitute ability[7]. The emphasis on activities rather than commodities does mean, however, that there is a danger of ignoring substitutes where different materials or processes are used (for example, steel versus plastic buckets). A sensitive and flexible approach is what is required rather than a blanket decision on the number of digits to be used.

We have already seen how Bain was very careful to use only well-defined industries. One implication of the foregoing remarks is that any empirical study in this area should be examined very carefully for the appropriateness of the industry definitions used.

The difficulties of using these official statistics (which were not designed principally with the structure-performance or competition policy practitioner in mind) has led some researchers to consider using other sources of data. One such source which has been well picked over by now, is the Profit Impact of Marketing Strategy (PIMS) data. This originated in a collaboration between an executive in General

Electric Inc. who believed in scientific management, and Harvard Business School. The units of analysis are business units, normally individual of parts of divisions of large corporations. The market definition is decided upon by discussion between the PIMS team and the management who then prepare answers to a number of questions on perceived relative product quality, market share, growth of market etc. involving a total approximately two hundred variables. To preserve confidentiality all the answers can be scaled up or down by any factor the respondents choose. The PIMS Institute then uses the results to give the respondent a comparison with other members facing similar market circumstances.

Since the PIMS data were set up for purposes of management consultancy they are no more ideal than Census of Production data. For one thing the sample is biased towards divisions of large companies with an interest in scientific management.

Secondly, for reasons of confidentiality, the market in which each "firm" operate is not disclosed, and neither is the firm's absolute size. Finally, some of the answers (for example on relative product quality or market share) are liable to be subjective and influenced by knowledge of financial performance. However these are different shortcomings from the Census data, so the PIMS programme may be useful in obtaining a view from a different angle.

The discussion so far has taken an implicit view of the firm as an enterprise engaged in one activity or selling to one market. Where divisions or plants are single-product or where the product-mix is similar within the "industry" this should not cause any particular problems. Where plants can easily switch the proportions of their outputs there is a justification for treating the whole output as part of the same industry. Unfortunately the quality of financial data is much better at company level. Presumably a plant or division uses some central corporate resources and there is always a problem of allocating these "overhead" costs through the company. Since they represent both private and social costs they should clearly be counted. This consideration has led some people (Shepherd, [168]) to argue for the use of company data in structure-performance work. This seems a feasible proposition provided that a sufficient breakdown is available of the company's activities to allow it to be treated as a composite line of business, operating in several markets.

Company accounting requirements laid down either by national law or accounting standards authorities frequently insist on some breakdown of financial accounts by activity. The results of this are of little use, however, because the large measure of discretion exercised by companies results in non-standard, vague and/or excessively aggregated classifications. For example, a study of conglomerates by the USA's Federal Trade Commission (FTC) made in the 1970s showed that, although the companies collected data on profits, assets etc. for over thirty categories, they only reported on average about five categories.[7]

In response to this, the FTC tried, through its line of business (LB) programme, to require 400–450 of the largest US corporations to report detailed income, expenses, assets, and supplementary accounting data assigned to 261 SIC-based manufacturing (and 14 non-manufacturing) industry categories. The programme met with stiff opposition on grounds of cost, difficulty in securing confidentiality, and the claim that economically meaningful profit rate for individual products could not be measured by their accounting systems. This may hide a simple and natural reluctance to be subject to outside scrutiny, whether for antitrust reinforcement or other reasons. In any event, the programme was scaled down to 450 companies and 267 lines of business, and eventually abandoned in 1977. Bentson [10] mentions 19 published reports on the basis of four years' data. (See, for example [151]).

Similar problems to those raised about the US data from conglomerates are felt in other countries. In addition, problems have arisen because some countries did not collect official data on the variables of interest. For example Phlips [144] had to compute concentration ratios from frequency distributions for Belgium, France, and Italy, and could obtain no concentration data for Germany in 1963. Although official data have improved considerably since then, US data even without LB is regarded as very good—for example, the available level of disaggregation is finer. This is one reason why studies for the USA greatly outnumber studies for all other countries combined.

---

[7] Comment by F.M. Scherer in Harvey J. Gold Schmid (ed). Business Disclosure: Governments Need to Know; New York, McGraw-Hill, 1979, p. 131.

3.2 Accounting data and economic concepts

Even where data can be obtained on a well-defined enterprise in a well-defined industry there are further problems of correspondence between theoretical constructs and the type of information.

A full competitive equilibrium for an industry involves two conditions—equality of marginal cost and price, which results from price-taking behaviour, and equality of price to the minimum attainable level of average cost, which results from the free entry assumption. Although this distinction is not usually made explicit, the empirical work can be divided according to whether its focus of interest is on the former or the latter condition. The latter is more in the spirit of Bain's original work. Rather than focus on price and average cost directly, however problems of index numbers and costs jointness which arise in multiproduct enterprises can be avoided by restricting analysis to profit rates. (Cubbin and Hall [53] examine time series data on prices and costs to investigate the effects of mergers. For other attempts to examine prices and costs directly see [126] (on gasoline) [123] (food chains) and [174] (newspaper rates.))

Apart from the problems of industry and firm definition outlined above there are a number of problems in defining a profit rate. The no-entry-barriers condition implies that the net present value (NPV) of an investment in an industry in equilibrium will be zero. This implies that the IRR will be equal to the cost of capital. Conversely, where supernormal profits are being earned the NPV should be positive and the IRR should be greater than the cost of capital. The difference between the IRR and the cost of capital would then be a measure of the degree of departure from a competitive equilibrium, which if it persisted might be attributable to market structure.

Now there are problems with calculating both the cost of capital and the IRR. First consider the cost of capital. In cross section work it is probably safe to ignore the problem of variation in interest rates over time. However, the return on, for instance, government stocks is only a base level for the cost of capital. Government stocks are generally held to be much less risky than industrial securities. The latter generally require risk premium.

3.3 Adjustments for risk

It is sometimes useful to distinguish between risk, where a basis exists for deriving probabilities, and uncertainty, where it does not. In the case of heavily traded securities the various probability distributions are fairly well established, so we may safely refer to the risk associated with a particular security. Following Markowitz [123] the risk of any portfolio is measured by its variance; largely because of its amenability to mathematical analysis.

The traditional approach, which examines the relationship between distribution parameters is epitomised by Fisher and Hall [76]. They regress mean returns on both the standard deviation and skewness (of firms over time) and use these coefficients to adjust industry profit rates for risk. Together these explain 16% of interfirm variation, and "risk premia" of up to 7 percentage points are observed.

They also examine an alternative measure of risk, namely intra-industry variation. This accounts for 73% of the variation in industry means and produces risk premia of up to 80%. This procedure obviously leaves less variance to be explained by structural variables. Caves and Yamey [24] argue with Winn [192] provides some empirical evidence that profit variability may be a by-product of oligopolistic behaviour in concentrated industries.

Hurdle [97] and Baker [7] examine another source of risk—namely financial leverage (which increases the temporal variability of equity returns and the probability of default). Again, however we are faced with the endogeneity of so-called exogenous variables. Hurdle finds that higher concentration results in lower leverage. Baker, however finds concentration has no strong separate effect on risk, but cost fixity leads firms to choose lower debt/equity ratios. Having corrected for this effect it does appear that for his sample higher leverage increases the returns to equity.

These "traditional" approaches to risk sit uncomfortably with more modern financial analysis, after the capital-asset pricing model (CAPM) of Sharpe [166] and Lintner [119]. This suggests that a security risk is measured not by its individual variance, but by its contribution to the variance of the portfolio in which it is held. Since unsystematic variance can (absent transactions costs) be diversified away simply by increasing the number of securities in the portfolio the significant aspect of a security's risk is the covariance of its returns with the returns of the other securities in the portfolio. In practice, this is generally measured by the regression slope coefficient (referred to as beta) obtained from regressing the coefficient security's returns on the market portfolio. There is a strong evidence that portfolios with higher aggregate "betas" will have higher returns. The evidence is rather weaker at the individual security level. One transactions costs are taken into account full diversification may not be optimal so the security's variance also may affect the cost of capital. There are a number of problems in applying the CAPM to accounting data. For example the returns of a security are defined in terms of dividends and capital appreciation. Thus a firm's riskiness depends on the stock market behaviour of its securities rather than directly on the characteristics of its earnings. True, some researchers have found a positive relationship between accounting and financial beta coefficients but the theoretical relationship between the two has yet to be fully spelt out. The number of studies examining returns on assets (which is the relevant measure for structure—performance studies) rather than securities which also take account of systematic risk is rather small, and results have tended to be of the expected sign only where the beta coefficient was multiplied by another variable such as the ratio of debt to equity [87] or capital-sales ratio [13]. Other studies [14], [54] and [131] have found negative coefficients of beta on rates of return. It is possible that in these studies beta was picking up unmeasured aspects of market power. Sullivan [178] found that large and concentrated firms had lower betas and hence lower capital costs.

Beta coefficients, according to the CAPM, measure riskiness in a statistical and *ex post* sense. Many investments of a pioneering nature which, with hindsight, look very sound may have been perceived, before the event, to be very risky. Unfortunately there seems to be no adequate means of measuring this type of risk, or as some would prefer to call it, uncertainty, even though one would expect uncertain investments to yield a higher mean return.

Even if such investments did not yield a higher return there would be a problem for statistical work. If one distribution of investments has a higher variance of outcomes than another, there will be a greater rate of disappearance through insolvency in the former group. Even if the distribution means are identical the lower tail of the higher risk category will be truncated and the mean of the surviving firms will tend to be higher. (Unpublished work by R.J. Allard, which examined the relationship between size of company and profitability on a large sample, found that correcting for the selection bias arising from the larger variance of small firms reduced but did not eliminate the negative relationship between size and profitability for UK companies.) Since most empirical work is carried out on surviving firms this phenomenon may be a source of distortion if this riskiness is correlated with measures of either concentration or barriers to entry.

Indeed, some critics of the SCP paradigm typically argue that most so-called supernormal profits are (if not the direct result of government policy) nothing but the reward for entrepreneurial superiority and willingness to take risks. In this view barriers to entry are simply an expression of this superiority and high concentration merely one way in which the rewards are reaped. If one adopts this as an *a priori* position there seems little point in carrying out any statistical work. Indeed no purely statistical results of inter industry analysis could refute this position, only detailed case studies demonstrating the tendency to monopolise in the absence of legal constraints. An example of this kind of work is [70]. The intra industry analyses of are also suggestive. It is ironic that the difficulties and biases of the single case-study approach are what led Bain to undertake inter-industry analysis in the first place.

3.4. *The Internal rate of return*

Apart from the cost of capital, the second element in measuring supernormal profit is the internal rate of return. This is almost never available (see Sampson [158] for an attempt to estimate internal rates of return from published data.) Accounting rates of return (ARR) are used instead as a substitute, and there is some argument concerning their suitability, Harcourt [93] showed that in general there is no simple relationship between the two and Stauffer [173] rigorously analysed the various conditions for biases in different directions, and carried out case studies simulating typical projects in a number of industries which showed a strong tendency for ARR and IRR to diverge. John Kay [107] independently discovered Stauffer's result that with a steady growth rate equal to the (constant) ARR, then IRR = ARR. Recently Fisher and McGowan [75] have produced a number of examples showing how different depreciation methods and growth rates produce, with identical values of IRR, different values for ARR depending on the company's growth rate, time profile of cash flows, and depreciation methods. These simulations may give a feel for the likely size of the problem, but until the calculations are carried out for actual companies the size of the problem is difficult to judge. Insofar as there is no systematic relationship between these biases and the RHS variables in the econometric work there should be no bias in the results and regression coefficients. However, for some sources of divergence between ARR and IRR there is an argument that the deviation is systematic.

To follow this argument it is necessary to say something about the reason ARR and IRR diverge. The problem arises from the treatment of capital expenditures, especially in regard to depreciation. In economic terms depreciation is the decline in the present value of an asset's future yields. For any projects this can be calculated *ex post.* At any moment in time the ratio (Net receipts minus economic depreciation)/(present value of asset) is constant and equal to the internal rate of return (provided that present value is calculated using the IRR as the discount rate.) Unfortunately accountants have to carry out their calculations before the end of the project and are forced to estimate depreciation, typically using some rule of thumb possibly modified by extraneous information. Discrepancies between economic and accounting depreciation will affect the numerator of the above expression, but in subsequent periods will also affect the estimate of the asset's present value. At the danger of oversimplifying, consider the case where the accountant writes off an asset too quickly. In the early years the numerator will be biased downwards, and later it will be biased upwards. As time progresses the denominator will become more biased downwards. In this case we have downward bias in the early years of the project, and an upward bias later on. In this case we are dealing with a ratio, however, these biases do not cancel out. In a steady state (with a new project commencing each period) more rapid depreciation will increase the ARR compared to IRR as long as the growth rate (g) is less than ARR. The bias goes the other way if g exceeds ARR since in this case the downward bias from the "new" proejects exceeds the upward bias from the "old" projects. Where g = ARR the two biases cancel out.

In response to Fisher and McGowan, Long [120] and Ravenscraft [150] and Martin [125] stepped in to defend to the practices of SCP econometrics. Between them they make several points including the following.

1) Imperfect measurement is not the same as "totally misleading" measurement.
2) Accounting and economic rates of return are likely to be quite highly correlated.
3) Other measurements besides ARR which do not suffer from the same problems are frequently used and generally give similar results.

Fisher and McGowan seemed to be concerned to defend IBM's profit record and were less concerned with bias in econometric analysis. The types of capital investment giving rise to worries about bias are those that appear on the RHS of SCP equations. (Bias arises if the error term, here taken to be ARR-IRR, is correlated with an explanatory variable.) These are advertising expenditure and Research and Development (R&D) spending, which are sometimes included to represent entry barrier variables. Advertising is typically treated by accountants as a current expense, and it is typically depreciated totally in the year of spending. (The treatment of R&D seems less uniform.) The argument against this is that both introspection and econometric estimates suggest that advertising has effects which last beyond the current year. To correct this some researchers have attempted to adjust profit and capital figures along the following lines:

$$\text{Adjusted profit rate} = \frac{\text{Net profits} + \text{current advertising} - \delta(\text{Goodwill})}{\text{Net assets} + \text{Goodwill}}$$

where Goodwill = present value of future benefits from advertising and δ=rate of decay of goodwill. Obviously if δ =100% this adjustment makes no difference. If, as is typically the case, the firm's growth rate is less than its ARR the effect of this adjustment in a steady rate is to reduce the apparent profitability of firms which advertise heavily. It is not surprising therefore that Ayanian [3], Bloch [1], and Reekie [153] find that this adjustment leads to a reduction in the apparent effect of advertising on supernormal profits.

This procedure is justified as long as the chosen depreciation rates are realistic. However, D.G. Clarke [34] argues that the degree of persistence of advertising is likely to be heavily overestimated. His starting point is the observation that the degree of persistence is typically measured by the regression coefficient on the lagged dependent variable in equations explaining sales by advertising (and other variables). He notes the curious fact that this coefficient seems independent of the frequency of observation. However, the decay rate cannot possibly be 10% per week *and* 10% per month *and* 10% per year, and he suggests that there is an upward bias due to serial correlation of errors in the presence of a lagged dependent variable. If Clarke's criticisms are valid it is likely that studies adjusting rates of return for advertising goodwill have carried their adjustment too far. Weiss [184] using a uniform 33% per annum decay rate finds that the adjusted profitability ratio is still related to advertising intensity. By conrast, Bloch's decay rate was only 5%. This rate was chosen to maximise the explanation of "variations in the relationship between the market value and book value of the stock of firms in the regression sample." Since this variable is sometimes regarded as a measure of the capitalised value of market power it is perhaps not surprising when the assumption of such a depreciation ration eliminates all the apparent effect of advertising on entry barriers. Reekie [152] differs from the other authors in assuming a linear depreciation schedule, and finds that the simple correlation between adjusted profitability and advertising/sales ratios turns from positive to negative for write-off periods greater than or equal to 3 years. The validity of any inferences concerning entry barriers from this kind of analysis is discussed elsewhere in this survey. These results were discussed here in order to demonstrate some of the problems in using accounting rates of return.

One attempt to escape problems arising from the ARR has been to make use of Tobin's q ratio (see [118] and [156].) Originally developed for use at the macroeconomic level for predicting investment cycles q is the ratio of the market value of a firm's assets to their replacement costs and corresponds to an inflation-adjusted version of Robin Marris's valuation ratio. Thus a valuation ratio above unity implies that any internal rate of return is greater than the appropriate discount rate for the firm. This also appears to sidestep rather neatly the problem of adjusting for different perceptions of the riskiness of assets, as the unknown discount rate is already incorporated into the market valuation. However, problems do still remain. The calculation of replacement value depends upon the choice of an appropriate price index for each item of capial good. More significantly, book values (whether inflation-adjusted or not) depend upon assumptions about depreciation to just the same extent as ARR measures.

Furthermore, relative q ratios for individual companies will depend upon both the size of the financial beta coefficient and the level of the stock market price index in comparison with its long term trend. At stock market peaks high beta coefficient firms will tend, on average, to show relatively higher valuations and vice versa, and this fact will introduce an element of noise into the dependent variable.

3.5 Choice of appropriate dependent variable

The discussion in the last section was deliberately vague in defining two related aspects of the rate of return. Whose income (profit) and whose assets should be used in calculating the profitability ratio (see section below below for alternatives to return on capital.) The straightforward answer would seem to be the firm's assets usually defined as fixed plus current assets minus current liabilities and equal to shareholders'capital plus long-term debt. The corresponding profit figure is profit net of depreciation and company taxation but before payment of interest on long term debt. Since the economic concept of a rate of return is an instantaneous one it seems that the most appropriate value of assets to use it the mean of the start-of-year and end-of-year values, although it is generally easier to take end-of-yaer values as they are invariably reported simultaneously with the year's earnings figures. The difference matters most with fast rates of positive (and more particular negative) growth.

A popular alternative (used in [66],[91])to the return on net assets is the return to shareholders equity. Hall and Weiss (p.231) have justified this on the grounds that this is what companies are assumed to maximise.

This does not, however, seem to be an adequate justification. The appropriate measure would seem to be the answer to the question, "what rates of return would be equalised in a competitive equilibrium?" Unfortunately as we have now seen in the last section, differential risk may mean that no *measurable* rates of return would be equalised. What is required is *either* a widely-accepted mechanism for correcting for risk or the inclusion of risk-determining variables as explanatory variables. The principal difficulty with the use of return on shareholders' equity is that yet another source of variation due to risk is added, namely variations in the choice of leverage. If, as some of the author quoted above suggest, this is related to market power, the use of the return on equity adds another source of random variation and of uncertainty regarding the correct specification.

There is general agreement that after-tax profits should be used. Companies vary in their tax liability, but suppliers of finance are interested in the after-tax returns, and it is these that would be equalised in a free-entry equilibrium.

A number of other problems with the return on capital should be noted briefly. First, there is the problem that assets are revalued at the present value of future returns, including any monopoly rents. Hard evidence on this is difficult to come by, but it is my impression that it is buildings and real estate which historically have been most subject to revaluation. Accounting requirements mean that these would typically be valued at not more than their open market price. The real problem seems much more likely to arise as a result of takeover. The purchase price in most cases exceeds the book value of assets. This excess will be a combination of allowance for inflation, for excessive depreciation, and capitalised monopoly profits (and some might say overoptimism on the part of the management of the "raiding" firm. See [73] and [128]).

One disadvantage of using rates of return is that it limits the units of analysis to those where asset figures are collected. In practice this tends to mean that entire companies are allocated to industries on the basis of their primary industry—a procedure which creates errors in measurement on both sides of the equation lowering explanatory power and biasing downwards regression coefficients. Imel and Helmberger [98] report on an attempt to reclassify firms in the food industry, but this reconstruction depended heavily on the co-operation of the companies concerned to obtain weightings for individual product sectors. This gives rise to worries about sample selection bias on non-replicability owing to confidentiality conditions imposed by co-operating companies.

Difficulties with company data are one justification for using data collected specifically by industry. Many countries engage in censuses of industrial activity (see section 3.1). Typically data on production sales, purchases by various category, wages, inventory changes, fixed investment, etc. are collected for individual plants (or some statistical approximation thereto.) Expediency dictates that the information requested is more or less limited to the type of data that a plant would need for its efficient operation. Furthermore some costs relevant to a plant may be incurred elsewhere, depending on the way the company is organised and the importance of services provided by any central office. Examples of these excluded costs may be selling and promotional expenditures (including advertising) and research and development. Nor is information collected on capital stock or depreciation. This precludes any examination of what we might call the *entry barrier equation,* involving rates of return on capital.

The variable actually used in studies employing this data is typically (value of sales (or production) minus directly attributable costs)/value of sales (or production). Since costs refer to production rather than sales it would seem appropriate to use production. Collins and Preston who pioneered this particular corner of the field used shipments (= sales) and the majority of other authors seem to have followed their example. Dividing numerator and denominator of the above expression by an index of the quantity of output produces the expression:

$$\frac{\text{average output price} - \text{average direct cost}}{\text{average output price}}$$

Average direct cost is almost certainly an underestimate of marginal cost. The distinction between short and long run marginal cost need not detain us, beyond noting that deviations of output from design output could be another source of error. Directly attributable costs include materials, direct labour, and fuel costs. The most obviously missing source of cost is the contribution of capital either in the short run (incremental wear and tear) or long run (costs or replacement) senses. One way out of this problem has been to add in as an explanatory variable the typical capital/sales ratio. If costs of capital were directly proportional to capital this would seem to be a reasonable adjustment; but long-lived investments (such as buildings) will have capital costs dominated by interest, whereas shorter lived capital will have a large depreciation element in costs; but this depreciation element seems largely ignored. For example, some sophisticated authors [12], have adjusted the raw price cost margins by subtracting r(K/pQ) from the calculated price cost margin. This only reflects the *interest* cost of capital. To take a proper account of capital a term like $(r + \delta)(K/pQ)$ should be used for adjustment, where δ is a typical depreciation rate specific to the industry. In any event, it seems that the problems of the measurement of capital and depreciation can not be avoided by a resort to price-cost margins rather than rates of return.

4. ECONOMETRIC PROBLEMS

Econometric problems arise because the data employed do not conform to the classical assumptions. The art of econometrics is in setting up a model and estimation procedure in such a way that these difficulties are obviated. The only econometric problem inter-industry analysis do not suffer from is autocorrelation. However, they more than make up for this in the severity of other problems, with which we deal in vaguely logical order.

Fixity of exogenous variables in repeated samples

The independent variables are not set by a disinterested experimenter, but are the result of a great many factors, including intervening variables likely to determine both structure and performance. This problem is not peculiar to inter industry analysis, and is particularly important in the current context as it has implications for the interpretation of causality.

Endogeneity of independent variables

Empirical studies generally show a high positive correlation between growth and profitability. The causation is generally believed to run from profits to growth, given managerial preferences and constraints on raising capital. If success breeds growth, monopoly profits are likely to be spent on increases in firm size both by diversification and growth in sales of a given product. [124] Alternatively, high profits can give rise to entry and thus lead to a reduction in market concentration. Thus there is a potentially a feedback from profitability to concentration. Similarly, there are potential feedback problems where advertising/sales is used to proxy barriers from "product differentiation" advantages. For this reason a number of studies have attempted a simultaneous equations approach. The general issue of endogeneity is treated in more detail in Section 6.4.

Measurement error

As the previous section has demonstrated, the correspondence between theoretical constructs and measures adopted in empirical work is frequently tenuous, partly because of difficulties in obtaining specific data, but also because theory does not always indicate a precisely appropriate measure. To take an example, the appropriate concentration measure may be a concetration ratio if some form of dominant firm model with a competitive fringe is correct, but a Herfindahl index measure if a Cournot-based theory is appropriate for all industries being considered. Measurement errors, as Weiss has pointed out, tend to reduce the apparent significance of the relationship estimated.

Specification error

This includes the omission of relevant variables correlated with included variables (leading to bias) the use of the wrong variables, and the choice of the wrong functional form. It is fairly standard practice to omit variables because of non-availability, despite the known consequences for parameter estimates. Since Bain's work there has been the tradition of a "critical concentration ratio" but empirical estimates frequently assume a continuous relationship. If behaviour really is dichotomous as White's [190] and Dalton and Penn's [141] analyses conclude pretty well unequivocally the majority of studies are seriously flawed.

However, arguably the worst specification error is the failure to allow for an interaction between entry barriers and concentration. Following Bain—and indeed, much of the subsequent theorizing—we should expect that in the hypothetical equation

$$\pi = \alpha + \beta C + u$$

the value of β should be zero for industries with free entry, low but positive for industries with moderate entry barriers and "high" only for industries with substantial barriers to entry. Furthermore we may expect that for atomistic industries if the resultant degree of collusion is zero, the height of entry barriers should have no independent impact on π, so that $\propto$ should be independent of β the height of entry barriers. Therefore if we were to estimate

$$\pi_i = \propto + \beta C + \gamma B + \delta C \times B + u$$

the maintained hypothesis should be that $\gamma = 0$ and $\delta > 0$. Unfortunately very few investigators report equations with $C \times B$, and many of those that do not seem to conclude that $\delta = 0$ and $\gamma > 0$. For example, Salinger (1984) uses advertising and research and development as his entry barrier variables and ignores scale economies. These are significant themselves, but not in interaction with concentration. As Salinger observes, in the absence of entry barriers any link between profitability and concentration is as likely to be due to Demsetz's [62] differential efficiency effect and it could be argued that studies which do not test the interaction term are of little value. If this is the case why are there so many studies in this category? One possible answer is the effects of journal selection bias, arising from the presumed fact that positive results are more publishable than negative results. Another possibility is that the number of industries with substantial entry barriers is really quite small, and if econometric attention were limited to these few it would be apparent that the number of observations is too small to obtain robust estimates. Whatever the reason, the failure to adopt the theoretically appropriate specification must undermine the traditional interpretation of such studies.

Multicollinearity

The biggest problem with collinearity is typically that between estimates of concentration and minimum efficient scale as a percentage of industry sales (used as a proxy for scale economy barriers). This makes the separate identification of the effects of concentration and scale barriers rather difficult. A similar problem arises when testing the "differential efficiency hypothesis", where market shares of individual firms are included together with market concentration in explaining firms' rate of return (typically at the line-of-business level.)

Heteroskedasticity

Variance of profitability diminishes systematically with company size, which in turn is likely to be related to concentration, but few studies make any allowance for possible heteroskedasticity, with consequent inefficient estimation, biased 't' statisics and possibly mistaken inferences. Heteroskedasticity can also arise from the use of the wrong functional form, for example. See [57].

This brief summary is sufficient to indicate that most inter-industry structure-performance studies suffer from grave econometric problems. This is an indication of the difficulty of the task, rather than an indictment of the practitioners. Given the magnitude of the problems the overall quality of econometric work is at least as good as in other fields of applied econometrics. If anything, the level of care with which data sets are assembled is generally somewhat higher than average.

5. THE DETERMINANTS OF MARKET STRUCTURE

The vast majority of empirical studies have been single equation models which have treated market structure as exogenous (exceptions include [23], [19] and [83]). Insofar as any of the explanatory variables are endogenous to the system the possibility exists of bias in parameter estimates. Moreover, if market structure is not exogenous this may well effect the interpretation of results. As we have seen, the advocates of the "efficiency hypothesis" argue that concentration and profitability are both determined by differential efficiency. Empirical work on the determinants of concentration is therefore of relevance to this central policy issue.

5.1 Determinants of concentration

The elements of structure can be divided into concentration and entry barriers. There is a reasonable quantity of empirical work on the determinants of market structure. By and large, however, it does not address itself directly to the efficiency hypothesis.

Technological determinants

Both structuralists and their opponents agree that the minimum efficient scale of production plays a part in determining concentration, and this is supported by the empirical findings (for surveys of which see [56] and [161]).

These technological factors have their main effect via the minimum efficient scale (m.e.s.) of plant-level operations—the word "minimum" reflecting the fact that long run average cost curves seem to be L- rather than U-shaped. The estimation of m.e.s. is carried out by one of four methods. The most direct and time-consuming method is to survey alternative best-practice production technologies at different scales and estimate the optimal cost of production for each technology. This is the so-called "engineering" approach (of whom one of the leading exponents is Pratten [148]). The reliability of this approach depends upon careful interpretation of interviews with production engineers; but in general is fairly good. The two major pitfalls are the inability to take into account intangible diseconomies, such as those arising from the greater strike-proneness of large plants, and the problem of product definition. Different technologies tend to produce goods with different characteristics. For example, bread produced in small bakeries is almost always superior to the mass-produced variety. Mass-produced items also tend, for better or worse, to be more homogeneous than the hand-made article. This differentiation of the product explains the survival of companies operating plants below the engineering estimates of minimum efficient scale.

The second method estimating minimum efficient plant size avoids this problem, since it depends on observing which scales of plant survive. Indeed, one variant of this approach is called the "survivor" method, developed by Stigler. This counts as efficient any interval of plant scales that are increasing, or at least not decreasing in their share of total output. Unfortunately, the results of survivor estimates seem inconsistent with the "engineering" approach, and frequently give very different results over different periods. Given the cost of engineering estimates of scale, and the uncertainties of the survivor approach, why not use a more direct method such as statistical cost analysis? Statistical cost analysis has tended to show that, contrary to the exposition of elementary mircoeconomic theory textbooks, cost curves tend to be L rather than U-shaped, a fact generally confirmed by the engineering approach. However, a major problem here has been the availability of suitable data for a sufficient number of industries. Those industries for which the data exist tend to have to be unconcentrated—or at least, to have low minimum efficient scales—in order to generate sufficient observations and this defeats the object of the exercise.

In an attempt to bypass this problem Fuss and Gupta [79] have used pooled cross section and time series data combined with an assumption of homotheticity to generate alternative estimates of m.e.s. cost disadvantage, and the shape of the cost curve. Their findings indicate that engineering estimates probably substantially overstate that m.e.s. whilst estimates based on actual plants (which may be smaller than the optimum) may perhaps understates m.e.s. The correlation between their cost function estimate of m.e.s. and the four firm concentration ratio was 0.63.

Given the difficulties and costs of the approaches outlined above, other statistical approaches have frequently been adopted to provide proxy measures of m.e.s. both in studies explaining structure and in structure-performance studies themselves. Weiss [186], Strickland and Weiss [177] and Hart and Clarke [94], for example adopt the notion, due to Florence [159] of a median plant size, defined such that half of the industry's output is produced in larger, and half in smaller plants. Several other authors have followed Comanor and Wilson's [41] measure which is the mean size of plants bigger than Florence's median.

There is one major difficulty with such statistical measures of m.e.s., in that they are by definition closely related to measures of plant concentration. Assuming that no plant is shared between two or more firms, plant concentration forms a lower bound on market concentration. Therefore, we should not be surprised if such measures provide a strong explanation for market concentration.

This point should not be taken too far, however. One of the predictions of the technological explanation of concentration is a similar pattern of concentration across different countries. There is some support for this in the international comparisons carried out by Bain, and by George and Ward [81], for example, who found some similarities in their lists of concentrated and unconcentrated industries (for example, automobiles, cement, and glass tend to be concentrated, textile industries, shoes and furniture to be unconcentrated.) Caves et al. [23], p.49) matched 85 industries between the U.S. and Canada and found correlation coefficients of 0.75 between both the 4 – and 8 – firm concentration ratios in the two countries.

Plant concentration and, by implication, technological scale effects do not tell the whole story. For example, the food industry in the U.K. is considerably more concentrated than in other European countries. This no doubt reflects taste differences amongst consumers, but also differences in the extent of multiplant operation, and hence the growth histories of the companies involved.

There almost certainly are common elements in the economics of multi-plant operation across countries—for example, in the automobile industry, the wish to provide a range of models across the size spectrum. On the other hand, differences can emerge because of different merger histories or differences in the level of artificial entry barriers.

Mergers

Mergers are one of the causes of increased concentration identified by Walshe [82], and by Hannah and Kay [92], amongst others. A fair summary of this literature would be that roughly half of the observed increase in concentration in post-war Britain was due to merger. This assumes that the measure of concentration being utilised is sensitive to the number of firms. Opponents of the view that mergers increase concentration have favoured inequality measures (such as the variance of log (size)) for which the effect of a merger may be to increase, decrease, or (in rare cases) even leave concentration the same. However, pure variance measures of concentration have not been justified by any model of oligopoly profits, and are therefore widely regarded as being of only incidental relevance to structure-performance relationships. Many of the anomolies found in British and European market structure comparisons could be traced to industries, such as food and drink, which had been particularly subject to merger activity.

For a series of comparative studies of the effect of merger see D. Mueller [130] J. Müller's [133] analysis of German manufacturing industries finds growth through merger as important as internal growth in maintaining a high level of concentration despite market growth.

Effects of entry barriers on concentration

The effect of entry barriers on concentration is assumed to be a dynamic one: higher barriers reduce the entry rate and are therefore one possible source of concentration reductions. Bain identified three main sources of entry barriers: absolute cost advantages, economics of scale in relation to market size and absolute capital requirements.

In large scale statistical work absolute cost advantages are treated as irrelevant in the vast majority of cases; this is consistent with Bain's own conclusions. Minimum efficient scale is, of course, an important element in the theory of entry barriers in addition to its direct technological effect. Its effect can, however, be offset by a sufficiently large increase in demand, making "room" for more plants including possibly those of an entrant. Most studies of the determinants of changes in concentration find the expected negative sign on this variable but it is significant at the 5% level in only about half of the studies surveyed for this article. A high industry growth rate is therefore no guarantee of lower deconcentration.

One interpretation of these results is that scale effects operate in conjunction with other barriers. Thus a high rate of growth in the market may not be enough to facilitate entry where buyer loyalty to existing sellers combines with a significant minimum efficient scale to increase the risks of entry to prohibitive level. What is more likely to happen is that, trade barriers and exchange rates permitting, new competition takes the form of increased import penetration, which until recently most studies have not corrected for.

Following the example of the early work product differentiation has been a favourite category of entry barrier examined in looking at the determinants of concentration. One difficulty has been that there is no consensus on either the meaning of the term or the best way to measure it.

Product differentiation *per se* (as defined, for example, by Chamberlin in his classic work) simply implies that buyers distinguish between one producer's goods and another's. Bain, however, refers to a product differentiation *advantage* which means in effect, a more favourable demand curve for incumbents than entrants. Product differentiation in the sense of Chamberlin is a necessary but not sufficient condition for this. Since there is a difficulty in observing buyers' preferences directly these are generally deduced.

For example, it is presumed that final consumers are more loyal to existing brands than producer-buyers. A simple rationale for this might be that producers normally buy on a much bigger scale and therefore find it worthwhile investigating the objective properties of their purchases. Secondly these "objective properties" are more relevant for producer goods than consumer goods, so that consumer may be more easily swayed by ambience or associations. These considerations therefore suggest a breakdown between consumer and producer goods. Within consumer goods, Porter has used the distinction between "shopping" and "convenience" goods, for similar reasons. Shopping goods, such as major appliances are similar to producer goods in that their objective qualities are essential and are worth the investment in investigation.

Another, and complementary, method of producing a product differentiation classification is through a subjective assessment of the importance of branding in each market. Thus convenience consumer goods may be further classified into low, medium, and highly differentiated products. A more objective method, but one with its own problems, is to use advertising (usually deflated by total sales) as a direct measure of product differentiation.

Scherer [162] adopts both the "classification" and "advertising/sales" ratio approach to product differentiation. He found that, amongst consumer products, the more highly differentiated showed the biggest concentration increase over the period 1947-72, although this was not necessarily true for shorter sub-periods. Similarly, the advertising/sales ratio was significant in explaining changes in concentration between 1947 and 1972, but not 1963-72.

Mueller and Rogers' [132] results for the same period support the theory that advertising in consumer goods industries is associated with an increase in concentration, and they show that television advertising seems particularly potent. (This is after allowing for growth of market sales, which has an insignificant negative effect.)

This might lead us to expect a positive relationship between the level of concentration and the level of the advertising/sales ratio. However, as a number of studies show, [20], [89], [179] and [177] advertising peaks at moderately tight oligopoly levels. With the emergence of one dominant firm the incentive to advertise is reduced and thus the concentration increasing effects tend to be self limiting. (For example, Cable's results suggested a maximum advertising intensity for a

Herfindahl index in the range 0.40–0.45).

It is clear from the above discussion that we should expect to find, at the very least, a certain amount of multicollinearity in the variables used in structure-performance studies which will cause difficulties in attributing explanatory power to particular variables. In particular, there seems to be a difficulty in many studies in separately identifying the effects of concentration and scale economies.

The issue of simultaneity will also arise, if any of the "explanatory" variables in ordinary least squares regressions is a function of profits. Furthermore, since the explanatory variables are interrelated the sumultaneity bias will in principle affect the coefficients on all explanatory variables. In particular, since entry (and therefore a fall in concentration) is a function of profits, the industry concentration level should be treated as endogenous. Furthermore, since optimal advertising is a function the price-cost margin thus should also be treated as an endogenous variable.

A number of studies have been carried out to test the simultaneity issue, of which a pioneering example was that of Strickland and Weiss, who used a three-equation model with advertising/sales, concentration and price-cost margins as dependent variables. They report that estimation by two stage least squares give similar results to ordinary least squares. From this one may be tempted to conclude that simultaneity bias is no great problem. However, there are doubts about whether Strickland and Weiss' system is identified. This being the case no proper inferences can be made, and simultaneous equation bias must be regarded as potentially present in most studies. The general effect of this bias would be to understate the effect of concentration, but overstate the effect of advertising.

6. THE MAINSTREAM TRADITION - EMPIRICAL RESULTS

As the previous sections have indicated the appropriate theoretical and practical specification of the structure-performance relationship is extremely difficult to get right. Even where economists agree to the appropriate theoretical variable this is frequently unobtainable in practice. Economic theory is of little help when it comes to a specification of functional form, and the underlying assumption of inter-industry analysis, that the same relationship between structure and performance holds, give or take a crude classification to producer/ consumer goods or shopping-convenience goods, is a heroic one. Even more heroic is the implicit assumption that the independent variables are set as part of a divine experiment. Given all these problems it is not surprising that the mountain of empirical outpourings only justify tentative conclusions. There are a number of questions that the data need to answer.

These are:

1) Is there a positive relationship between concentration and profitability?
2) Are entry barriers important? If so which ones.
3) What is the effect of using different measures of profitability as performance measures?
4) Does simultaneity affect the issue?
5) Are monopoly profits transient?

This section attempts to answer these questions in turn.

6.1 Is there a positive relationship between concentration and profitability?

The answer to this is a qualified "Yes". Several hundred studies have been carried out for the United States and rather fewer for other countries. The US results have tended to be more straightforward because until the late seventies at least i) the data were better and ii) the US market in most goods was largely self-contained so there were not problems due to the effects of exports on performance, imports on concentration and entry barriers, or varying levels or tariffs. By contrast much of the work on performance, Canada, for example, has been concerned more with trade barriers than with concentration per se. [Caves et al. [23]]

Even for the US, however, there are several qualifications. Firstly, the effect of concentration is quantitively quite small in interindustry analysis and represents only a modest elevation of price above the "competitive" level for even the most concentrated industries, to an extent that is quite inconsistent with the elementary textbook version of monopoly; even after allowing for distortions arising from measurement and specification errors the price elation seems unlikely to be greater than about 10%; X-efficiency considerations might, at most, add another 5–10% on to these margins, and this is consistent with the orders of magnitude found in most intra-industry studies (except Thompson [181] who found a 42% rise in advertising rates for monopolistic provincial Irish newspapers and Lamm [111] who found a very small effect for retail food).

Secondly, the interindustry results became much more tenuous following the commodity and oil price shocks of the mid 1970s, and appear to be generally weaker in periods of rapid inflation. This is consistent with one version of the much-disputed administered pricing hypothesis.

The straightforward explanation for these results is that, in most markets there is a limit to the height of entry barriers of the order of 10–20%, but occasionally higher. Price is not elevated above these levels for fear of precipitating entry, a discrete phenomenon which may have a permanent effect on profitability. An subsidiary hypothesis is that beyond this level pressure on management to raise profits is attenuated, but this argument cannot really stand up on its own to scrutiny. If there were enormous unrealized potential for raising profitability this would imply a degree of imperfection in the market for corporate control at which even the most dedicated managerialist would baulk.

6.2 Are entry barriers important? If so, which ones?

Entry barriers, where they exist, seem important in limiting the potential for raising price. Since few of the many studies took as much care as Bain in specifying concentration and barrier effects as interacative this causes some problems of comparison.

Nevertheless, Bain's main conclusions are still generally supported by the mass of results. (It must be said, however, that there are some differences of interpretation). Since Bain's negative finding, absolute cost advantage as a barrier has not been investigated.

The main sources of entry barriers seem, firstly, economics of scale. There is a consistent positive relationship between the minimum efficient scale of operation as a proportion of industry output and industry profitability. However, this measure is highly correlated with absolute capital requirements so it is unusual to find both m.e.s. and capital requirements significant. A more sophisticated version first used by Caves et al. based on the "cost disadvantage ratio" seems also to be more robust. If forced to choose between the economies of scale and market crowding argument and the absolute capital requirements explanation the balance of the argument lies with the former. The latter requires moderately serious imperfections in the capital market and would seem to imply higher rates of profit on average firms which is not consistent with the known facts. However, it should be noted that trade possibilities undermine production-based scale economies. Low tariffs and transport costs, if combined with no major size advantages for marketing and international homogeneity of tastes, can bring foreign competition based either on a large local domestic market or even export based volume production.

If scale economies represent the main source in incumbent strategic advantages on the cost side, advertising, brand loyalty, product quality, and innovation represent the advantages on the demand side. Like the cost side advantages these are difficult to disentangle, as there is no completely satisfactory measure of product quality, innovation or even brand loyalty that can be consistently applied across markets in interindustry studies. Whilst Bain employed a subjective measure of product differentiation advantage, later researchers (following Comanor and Wilson) have tended to rely on advertising as the measure of demand side advantage, and there appears to be a highly stable positive relationship between profitability and industry advertising intensity, at least for consumer goods even within simultaneous equations studies. As we discuss elsewhere, thus probably represents a mixture of:-

i) real of imagined product advantages
Product advantages provide a basis for advertising copy and may signal to the consumer the producers faith in his product. Whether the advantage derives from chance or past investments superior products are likely to have a gross higher margins which will increase the incentive to advertise.

ii) the existence of market niches/monopolistic competition
When product differentiation is viewed in terms of spatial analogies ("horizontal differentiation") we may have a situation of local monopoly without the long run Chamberlin zero-profit equilibrium. In such cases advertising may occur to change consumer "location" (ie tastes) or producer "location" (ie consumer perceptions) to persuade

otherwise indifferent consumers to buy one's own product.

iii) advertising as a pure entry barrier
This can act to raise capital requirements, M.E.S. and to create threats of post-entry advertising wars [51]. More detailed work on each of these components is needed to sort out their relative importance.

The third major source of entry barriers is government regulation, which may effect entry directly or indirectly through, for example, licensing requirements or restrictions on advertising. Studies of the effects of advertising restrictions show price effects of at least 25% in eye glasses [9] and between 4% [21] and 34% [155]. Deregulation of intercity bus routes in Britain produced a fall in fares and the effects of US airline deregulation on price and service levels are well known. (Successful deregulation in this sense, however, requires that competitive, or at least, contestable, conditions are available following deregulation).

6.3 The effect of using different profitability/performance measures

Liebowitz [116] questions Collins and Preston's finding of a high correlation between "price cost margins" and accounting rates of return, and with an alternative data set finds correlation coefficients mainly in the region 0.2–0.4 even after adjusting for capital intensity. Once advertising intensity is allowed for these correlations weaken even further.

If there results are accepted Liebowitz claims that they undermine the rationale for all studies employing price-cost margins, but only if one regards price-cost margins and rates of return as interchangeable variables—which some authors do not. Nevertheless, Liebowitz's paper does suggest why different results are sometimes obtained using price-cost margins rather than accounting rates of return, and justifies caution in interpreting results based on gross margins.

Different versions of accounting rates of return, however (trading profits/gross assets or profits after interests/equity, pre- or post-tax) tend to give similar results, except where advertising is treated as a capital good and depreciated extremely slowly. In most cases the choice of dependent variable is dictated by considerations of data availability which means a choice of either rates of return or price-cost margins. All the UK and Australian studies to date, because they have been based on the Census of Production rather than company level data have used margins, so no comparison is possible. By contrast all the Japanese studies surveyed by Weiss in 1974 used rates of return on equity, so again no comparison is possible. The US experience, however, seems to be that the same variable appear as significant whichever dependent variable is used.

6.4 Simultaneity

Studies employing a simultaneous approach include [177], [125], [139], [23], Phillips [142] and Geroski [82]. One of the major problems which arises once the simultaneity issue is faced is the shortage of truly exogenous variables which may be crucial in ensuring identifiability of the system. However, any criticisms along these lines are relevant *a fortiori* to single-equation studies. Typically three-equation models are employed, with profitability, advertising, and concentration as the three dependent variables although Connolly and Hirschey [42] for example employ a fourth equation for research and development. The latter were also unusual in testing explicitly for simultaneity, the results which were mixed.

The main effect of allowing for simultaneity appears to be that the concentration ratio becomes rather less significant in the profits equation, but the advertising/sales ratio is unaffected. It is not obvious how to interpret this finding, however. More analysis of simultaneity issues would be welcome.

6.5 Are monopoly profits transient?

This is one of the central policy questions. The notion of workable competition which is implicit in much of the approach to policy does not view supernormal profits themselves as a symptom of harm, since they may represent a return to entrepreneurial activity which typically also produces benefits to consumers and producers. Indeed the patent laws are designed to grant temporary monopoly profits as a reward for innovation. However, a permanent divergence of price from the opportunity cost of resources employed and the concomitant loss of beneficial trading opportunities are another matter. (As an example, consider a world where IBM had not adopted an open architecture for its personal computer and had managed to remain the sole supplier of PC-type hardware. Prices would have remained high, many fewer would have been sold, and software prices would probably also have stayed at a higher level for longer). There is no single answer for the optimal longevity of entrepreneurial profits which best balances out these considerations (see [137]), but in the vast majority of cases a reasonable upper limit would seem to be a 15–20 years; certainly there is little support for an extension of patent life beyond 20 years.

Yale Brozen [18] argued that the period covered by Bain's work was unrepresentative and was a period of disequilibrium and supported his argument, by showing a tendency to falling profitability amongst Bain's high concentration—high profit firms. However, given any random component of profitability we should show some regression towards the mean, and the critical question is how quickly. Qualls [149] and Mueller's [129] studies both showed a great deal of persistence. In Qualls' study this was particularly the case for high entry barrier industries. An ambitious international comparative study to be published in 1988 extends Mueller's work for individual firms, using an autoregressive model proposed by Geroski. Within these samples contain firms from industry with high, low, and no entry barriers. In another study looking at the persistence of concentration Shaw and Simpson [167] showed that in the UK high market shares tend also to be persistent.

Over the longer term (say 50–60 years), of course technological progress and structural change combine to reduce the importance of particular monopolies, but if monopoly levels persist beyond 15–20 years this potentially implies a period of 30 or more years of resource misallocation.

7. CONCENTRATION, WAGES AND UNIONIZATION

One strand of thought which we have not referred to elsewhere represents a possible source of bias in structure performance studies. It is generally recognised that trade unions manage to raise wages. Both wages and unionization are higher in concentrated industries for fairly obvious reasons (concentrated industries are easier to organise; if entry barriers are present competition from non-union labour can be prevented). Although the possibility of passing on wage increases to the consumer may be equal, given the elasticity of final product demand, in both concentrated and atomistic industries, the threat of entry of a non union firm is much less in the latter, particularly if the high concentration is due to scale economies.

This idea has traditionally foundered on the empirical results (such as [185]) which show that, once labour force characteristics have been allowed for, there is no apparent wage discrepancy in concentrated industries. These "labour force characteristics" include not only obvious "quality" variables like years of schooling, but also physical characteristics such as race and gender. If it is also true that unionised/ concentrated industries have discriminated against women and racial minorities the coefficients on these characteristics would be biased. Recently a few studies have returned to this question. Jenny [103] finds a positive effect of concentration on wages in France. Clark, for example, finds that in his PIMS-based sample [33] unions reduce company profitability for firms with market shares of less than 10% but not for high-market share firms. Thus although unions on average affect profitability, high market share firms seem to be able to either pass on wage increases or make counteracting productivity gains. By contrast Dowrick [68] finds that in the UK "bargained wage premia are deducted directly from profits rather than being passed on," and this is perhaps consistent with the more open nature of the British economy.

8. MARKET STRUCTURE AND PERFORMANCE – THE KEY ISSUES

The foregoing discussion implies that the estimation of structure-performance relationships is extraordinarily difficult and full of pitfalls for the unwary. It is impossible to collect data on all the relevant variables and the data that are collected rarely correspond to the theoretically appropriate measurement. Once the measurements have been taken and relationships estimated there is the problem of the robustness of the results to changes, not only in econometric specification, but also in sample definition. For example, the exclusion of one or two industries from Cowling and Waterson's sample was sufficient to destroy the statistical significance of concentration increases in their results (see Hart and Morgan [95]). But what are we to conclude from this? By eliminating variation in the independent variables one can always destroy the statistical significance of regression results.

It is clear from a wide reading of such empirical work that the better the data set and the more care taken in its construction the more likely is a positive effect of concentration on profitability to emerge. For example, the British data, which are much more affected by import competition, produce much less robust structure-performance relationships than U.S. data. The latter is superior in many other respects too, such as more complete disaggregation, and the availability of line of business information. Furthermore the data has been more thoroughly reworked to iron out problems of industry definition.

The fundamental issues underlying all the work is the nature of the market economy—in particular the extent to which pockets of monopoly can exist and if so, the extent to which these are associated with high concentration. Ultimately these have implications for the conduct of a range of public policies from the treatment of horizontal mergers to decisions about regulation of public utilities and natural monopolies. However, until recently the policy issues were typically regarded as implicit or self-evident. A positive effect of concentration on profitability was regarded as implying the need for a tough stand against horizontal mergers (in the U.S.) whereas the apparent absence or weakness of such a relationship was regarded as justifying a continuation of Britain's permissive attitude to such mergers (for example in the official discussion document usually referred to as the Leisner report [117].)

However, more recently the traditional interpretation of such relationships has been challenged, most notably by Demsetz [61] and [62]. The argument is that the traditional approach fails to take into account the differential efficiency of firms either on the cost side or in their ability to meet consumer requirements. Greater efficiency in either or both senses would be expected to lead to both greater market shares for such firms and greater profitability. High market shares lead, of course, to greater concentration and therefore Demsetz argues that it is plausible that the observed relationship is due to an intervening variable. It would be wrong to split up dominant firms (as was being proposed in the Hart Bill at the time Demsetz was writing), therefore for two main reasons. The first is that any economies of scale would be lost, and the second is that the existence of such a policy would create adverse incentives in a market economy. Demsetz supported his argument by showing that small firms did not share in the benefits from high concentration enjoyed by larger firms. By implication, concentration is not a "shared asset" but a reflection of superior performance by the so-called dominant firms.

The force of Demsetz's argument is reflected in the fact that the thrust of much recent work has been to test this theory. Before we discuss these tests, however, an important point must be made. Demsetz's data refers to an economy in which horizontal mergers were, to all intents and purposes, banned for several decades. In such a setting high market share is indeed evidence of success at attracting customers. An argument which opposes the breaking up of dominant positions thus acquired is not an argument for a policy of allowing mergers. The British experience is that the latter is a means of gaining market share without lower prices or better quality. Whilst there is no evidence of immediate monopoly exploitation by merging companies, their lacklustre performance, and indeed the virtual destruction of some industries which had relied on merger as a means of solving what were essentially management problems, should cause other countries to consider carefully before they reverse a presumption against horizontal mergers. Indeed, when Clarke, Davis and Waterson [37] carried out a test on U.K. data similar to that carried out by Demsetz they found no evidence to support the Demsetz hypothesis. Differentials between large and small firms were smaller in concentrated industries and the latter were more profitable, thus supporting the notion of concentration as a "shared asset".

The initial response to Demsetz's challenge was to point out that high profits in a "monopolised" industry could tend to attract entrants, but if these could not overcome barriers to entry they would earn only normal profits, and would typically remain small and marginal. Thus the existence of a competitive fringe is quite consistent with the structure-performancee paradigm. Leonard Weiss [187], (p.225) proposed that:

> "The correct test for the hypothesis that high concentration merely reflects high market shares which derive from the same source as high profits would seem to be a study that takes market share and concentration into account at the same time. Market share should capture the effects of economies of scale, superior products, or superior

> management—and then some. At least in the case of dominant firms, it would also show the effect of control over price. If there is any effect for concentration, this would surely reflect the ability of concentrated industries to act collusively. Indeed, the effect of concentration would probably be understated, since market shares of leading firms and concentration are sure to be correlated."

Such testing had to await the availability of the line of business data set. Several unpublished papers were produced within the Federal Trade Commission. Ravenscraft (1973) was one of the first published studies using line of business data to address this issue. He found that, once market share was taken into account the coefficient on concentration turned negative and, in one equation, was marginally significant. An alternative specification involving an interaction term between concentration and market share produced a significant negative coefficient on this variable but insignificant coefficients on the non-interacted variables. This suggests that a single dominant firm with a large competitive fringe is better off than a concentrated oligopoly. As always, there is room for alternative interpretations of these results. However, they appear to lend more support to the efficiency hypothesis than they do to the traditional structure-performance report.

However, to judge by a recent paper by Haid and Neumann [90] the whole procedure of testing for efficiency effects may itself give rise to bogus results. In a simulation experiment they constructed various samples of firms and industries where the number of firms in the industry varied. These industries were set up with Cournot quantity setting behaviour and blockaded entry so that the effective degree of (price) collusion was related to industrial concentration. They also included some differential firm efficiency effects due to different marginal costs.

Despite the presence of market concentration effects which were picked up when market share was excluded, the inclusion of a market share variable produced insignificant coefficients on the market structure variables. If we can extrapolate from these results the apparent insignificance of concentration variables in the LB analyses may well be due to a similar effect. This would imply that, in a sense, market share is a better measure of market power than the traditional measures of concentration.

One major weakness of the LB data it its restriction to a particular time period. (Ravenscraft's data refer to 1975). Whilst this is generally a problem with any single-period cross section the abandonment of the LB data collection exercise means that tests over the business cycle will not be possible. It had already been established (for example Weiss, [187]) that there are important cyclical effects in the concentration-profits relationship, and it has been argued that the effects of the oil price stock hit concentrated industries disproportionately. This would distort all estimated structure-performance relationships for the mid seventies.

Evidence for this proposition is provided in the paper by Domowitz, Hubbard and Petersen [66]. Using newly-constructed panel data on 284 U.S. 4-digit industries they found a dramatic narrowing of the spread between the average price-cost margins of concentrated and unconcentrated industries, particularly over the 1970s. Although they found increasing import penetration to make a significant contribution to this decline, the major cause was found to be the effect of changing aggregate demand. Price cost margins in concentrated industries were more pro-cyclical than in unconcentrated industries even after taking into account variations in capital intensity. The authors postulate more flexible prices and/or more sticky costs in concentrated industries.

An earlier paper by Neumann, Bobel and Haid obtained a similar result using German data. In general they found a positive and significant effect of concentration on price cost margins, but the statistical significance of this declined during recession years. This is consistent with Domberger's finding that more highly concentrated U.K. industries adjust prices more quickly in response to inflationary pressures. (Only a limited amount of research has been done directly on this topic and the evidence is, as usual in economics, conflicting.) The traditional "administered pricing" hypothesis would have prices in concentrated industries less responsive. On the other hand models of collusive oligopoly behaviour such as Stigler's, or more recently Green and Porter's, would imply greater cartel instability at times of low demand. This would be consistent both with casual observation of OPEC, for example, and the results of Domowitz et. al.

A recent test of cyclical price flexibility was carried out by Farber [72] with 53 U.S. 5-digital industries over the period 1952-62. He found a robust U-shaped relationship with a turning point at a 4-firm concentration ratio of 62-64%. Industries in this region had a minimum rate of increase in transactions prices during upturn and a maximum incease (or minimum decrease?) during downturns—after allowing for variations in capital intensity. On the basis of this evidencce oligopolies showed the least price flexibility. However, by the standards of the 70s and 80s Farber's period of study is one of mild recessions. Such evidence as we have from the structure-performance studies suggest that this is not likely to be a general result.

As the matter now stands, it appears that the LB data available happen to be for years which are least favourable for the concentration hypothesis. A long run of such data would have been invaluable in sorting out this question. As things now stand the traditionalists remain unconvinced that the efficiency hypothesis can explain observed structure-performance relationships, and the efficiency school are convinced that it can.

One way to resolve this question of statistical inference in the presence of strong prior beliefs is to adopt a formal Bayesian methodology. A procedure for doing so has been suggested by Leamer [114] and Bothwell, Cooley, and Hall [14] report on an attempt to carry out this procedure for U.S. firm level data from the period 1960–67. In the presence of specification uncertainty traditional hypothesis tests are inappropriate, since the alternative hypothesis rarely amounts to the exclusion of a simple variable or set of variables, (with other coefficients held constant) but typically encompasses a wide range of possible values for the coefficients on variables which are not of immediate interest.

Bothwell et al. assign a prior value of zero to these other variables and calculate in turn confidence intervals for each of the ten variables used in their analysis, including measures of concentration scale economics, firm size, market share, and risk.

The most robust coefficients were those on advertising and market share, with firm growth and scale requirements also having strictly positive confidence intervals. With this data set and methodology the concentration variable had very wide confidence intervals, suggesting a wide range of specifications where the coefficient would be zero or negative. The conclusion they offer is a counsel of caution in the acceptance of empirical results.

A different approach is taken by Schmalensee [163] in a recent study of the 1975 LB data using an analysis of variance. Starting with a general "maintained" hypotheses of the simultaneous existence of industry, firm, and market share effects he sequentially tests restrictions on this general model. The existence of firm effects (i.e. effects common across several LBs) was decisively rejected; industry effects were found to be important and although market share effects were found to exist they accounted for only a negligible fraction of the total variance of business units rates of return, despite their statistical significance. Schmalensee's work is purely descriptive, however—"industry effects" include differential demand shocks and secular trends, as well as the more traditional structural variables.

The failure to find "firm" effects is surprising and casts doubt on the notion of good managerial qualities being spread across several business units. Combined with the existence of independent market share effects this suggests the importance of a strong element of chance in the determination of both market share and LB profitability, or the random distribution of managerial talent.

9. THE PERSISTENCE OF MARKET POWER AND PROFITABILITY

Most of the work to date on profit rates has used accounting data of one kind or another. An implicit (and sometimes explicit) assumption is that these accounting data contain information on long-run rates of return or profit margins, and that the data used will on average reflect the underlying long run rate of return. We have already seen that there may be cyclical effects on the concentration-profits relationship which implies that any one year's cross-section may give misleading results, but most researchers have been content to deal with this problem by at most averaging over several years (where the data permit.)

A pioneering effort to consider the issue of long run profitability was carried out by Brozen [17] and [18] whose maintained hypothesis was of a competitive environment which would not permit persistently high levels of profitability. Brozen found a tendency of Bain's high profit-rate industries to decline. From this he concludes that high profits are a disequilibrium phenomenon and are therefore a poor basis for policy—in particular, a proposed policy of divestment and deconcentration.

The crucial question for positive economics and for policy purposes is the speed with which the competitive mechanism is supposed to work, and whether the dynamics of the system converges to a competitive equilibrium.

Mueller's [130], work is directed towards answering these questions. This involved dividing his sample of 472 firms into 8 equal sized groups on the basis of their rankings in each of 24 years within the sample period, and examining the probability of transition from one group to the next.

The probability of a firm in the most profitable group still being there in the long run (i.e. asymptotically) is 0.34, much higher than the 0.125 figure predicted by the "competitive environment" hypothesis. This was also true of other above-average octile groups.

Furthermore, Mueller calculated long run rates of return (normalised by year effects) using the regression equation:

$$\pi_t = \propto^1 + \beta_{i/}t + \mu_{it}$$

$\propto$ gives the long run rate of return, and this was found to be substantial and significant for the extreme four octiles indicating a great deal of persistence.

These long-run profit rates then formed the basis of a substantial study (1986) which examined their relationship to several sets of variables reflecting the traditional concerns of industrial organisation, including the effects of corporate control, mergers, advertising, risk, patenting activity, and so on. Mueller concludes that although market concentration is a relevant (and statistically significant) factor, firm-specific variables (including variables involving market share) contribute more to the overall explanation than do industry effects (in apparent contradictions of Schmalensee's results reported above). Further evidence on both the degree of persistence and the determinants of long run profit rates and the speed of adjustment can be found in [56] and in a forthcoming volume (edited by Mueller) containing an international comparison of the same model across several countries.

10. SUMMARY AND CONCLUSIONS

We started this monography by questioning the relevance of the competitive model to the analysis of industry. Possible deviations from the competitive norm are important from the perspectives of both the modeller (whether micro- or macro-oriented) and the policy maker. Much of this paper has concerned itself with the difficulties involved in using cross section evidence to draw general conclusions about the way industrial markets operate.

Many different researcers have attempted to grapple with these problems; at best they have succeeded in dealing with one or two at a time. Weighing the imperfect evidence from these studies is bound to be a somewhat subjective affair, and so the reader is advised to treat the following observations with care.

The overall impression that emerges from an assessment of the studies mentioned in this paper is that the traditional structure—performance paradigm is basically correct, that high entry barriers combined with high concentration lead to supernormal profits, some of which may be absorbed through managerial discretion, X-inefficiency and so forth, and which may persist for economically significant lengths of time. Even the lowest available estimates of the resultant static welfare loss suggests there is a need to maintain some policies directed at sustaining a competitive environment.

However, the challenge of the efficiency hypothesis has caused some modification of the public policy stance associated with the traditional view. In particular, high concentration in the absence of substantial entry barriers is now regarded as much less of a source of problems, particularly where concentration has been attained through the success of internal expansion. As a corollary more attention is being paid to inter-firm, intra-industry differences in performance.

The static welfare losses, however, are probably small in comparison with the dislocating effects which occur when barriers to competition are eventually breached, either by foreign competition (which can easily decimate an industry, as U.S. and European car companies have found to their cost) or by radical changes in technology which circumvent the monopoly situation (as printing workers in the U.K. have recently discovered). There may be important benefits of a competitive industrial structure in spreading out the process of adjustment to structural and technologies changes.

Although the existence of structurally imperfect markets is important, much more than market structure is involved in determining company profitability. Company characteristics do appear to matter; management quality and/or luck should make a difference to productivity, to product quality, and to the choice of an appropriate set of products. The processes by which firms compete (even within imperfect markets) are, to anyone who has studied individual markets in depth, crucial to understanding industrial company and, indirectly, industry performance.

On a theoretical level it emerges that the Cournot model is far too naive to be more than a reference point for other models. Profits are not as closely related to concentration as the model would indicate. A theoretical model useful for explaining the course of prices in an industry has to include the possibility of discontinuous jumps. Recent developments focussing on the problem of maintaining collusive (partial or full) levels of prices in the face of demand fluctuations seem to be heading in a fruitful direction. This is a vast improvement on the situation twenty years ago when the only professionally respectable theory of the firm was a perfectly competitive one. If this is one of the legacies of all the hard work that has gone into the empirical analysis of structure and performance it will not have been in vain.

Underlying much of the academic debate has been disagreement on policy prescriptions, and this paper would not be complete without an assessment of policy implications. Although the evidence on matters of detail is not conclusive I believe the following policy points are robust to changes in perspective likely to be brought about by more refined empirical work.

1. Concentration and mergers. Where horizontal mergers are prohibited, (as in the USA before 1979) market share is determined largely by differential efficiency. Concentration will be the outcome of differential efficiency, scale effects, and luck. It would therefore not normally be appropriate to force the break up of dominant firms who have achieved dominance through internal growth.

   Where horizontal mergers are permitted large size and market share may be due in part of superior efficiency but past take over behaviour is the dominant influence. Indeed, the higher average efficiency of takeover predators is balanced by the average inefficiency of the “victims”. This lack of efficiency makes such companies particularly susceptible to new competition, whether from technological change or overseas competition.

2. Barriers to entry. These include three elements which have different policy implications- i) "natural" barriers, such as scale economies which may imply a regulatory option to be exercised. ii) strategic entry barriers such as the ability to carry predatory pricing or advertising. This can only be successfully proved in a small minority of cases, and the best defence is a competitive environment encouraged by strict merger and trade policy. iii) competitive advantage arising from a firm's long experience in a market, consumer loyalty, or particular skills. There are few or no rational grounds for attacking these advantages, the returns to which provide the motive power for the engine of industrial growth.
3. Profitability and dominance. It follows that neither profitability nor dominance should be attacked *per se* but only where found together with evidence of inefficiency, monopolisation, or predatory activities.

Where should future research be heading? As always, better data, better modelling, and better econometrics are likely to increase our understanding of the complexities of industrial organisation. However, the econometric approach to the subject has had some costs. There is a danger that we will know a lot in abstract about structure-performance relationship in general and nothing about any industries in particular. This is not a plea to go back to single-industry case studies but rather to take a cross section of several markets and study just one aspect of behaviour in case-study detail throughout the cross section. I believe this is the way to improve our knowledge of the details of the behaviour of industrial markets, whether we are interested in pricing, advertising, quality change, research and development, or strategic entry barriers.

Acknowledgements

I should like to thank Joan McSweeney and Kathryn Duff for their typing, Michael Cronshaw for his assistance with proof reading the manuscript and Melbourne University for financial support and a good working environment in the later stages of this project. I am grateful to Dick Allard, Paul Geroski for their comments and especially the editor of this section, Alexis Jacquemin, for his comments, suggestions and encouragement. Any remaining errors and omissions are, as usual my own responsibility.

Bibliography and References

[1] Armour, and Teece, "Organisational Structure and Economic Performance: A Test of the Multidivisional Hypothesis", *Bell Journal of Economics and Management Science,* pp 106–122 (1970).

[2] Axelrod, R., *The Evolution of Co-operation,* New York, Basic Books. 1984.

[3] Ayanian, R., "Advertising and Rate of Return", *Journal of Law & Economics,* 18, pp 479–506 (1975).

[4] Bailey, E.E., D.R. Graham and K.P. Kaplan, *Deregulating the Airlines,* Cambridge MIT press, 1985.

[5] Bain, J.S., "Relation of profit rate to industry concentration", *Quarterly Journal of Economics,* 65 (c), pp 293–324 (1951).

[6] Bain, J.S., *Barriers to New Competition,* Harvard University Press, Cambridge, Mass. (1956).

[7] Baker, Samuel H., "Risk leverage, and profitability: An Industry Analysis", *Review of Economics and Statistics,* tt (November), pp 503-7 (1973).

[8] Baumol, W.J., J.C. Panzar and R.D. Willig, *Contestable Markets and the Theory of Industry Structure,* New York, Harcourt Bruce Jovonovich, 1982.

[9] Benham, L., "The Effect of Advertising on the Price of Eyeglasses", *Journal of Law and Economics,* 15, pp 337–52 1972.

[10] Benston, G.J., "The Validity of Profits-Structure Studies with Particular Reference to the FTC's hire of Business Data", *American Economic Review* 75(1), pp 37–67 (1985)

[11] Bloch, Harry, "Advertising and Profitability: A Reappraisal", *Journal of Political Economy,* 82 (March/April), pp 267–86 (1974).

[12] Bothwell, James L., "Profitability, Risk and the Separation of Ownership from Control", *Journal of Industrial Economics,* 28 (3), pp 303–312 (1980).

[13] Bothwell, J. and T. Keeler, "Profits, Markets Structure, and Portfolio Risk", *Essays in Industrial Organisation in Honor of Joe S. Bain,* R. Masson and P. Qualls (eds.), Ballinger, Cambridge, Mass. 1976.

[14] Bothwell, J.L., T.F. Cooley and T.E. Hall, "A new view of the Market Structure-Performance debate", *Journal of Industrial Economics,* 32(4), pp 397–418

[15] Boyer, M., and M. Moreaux, "Consistent versus non consistent conjectures in Duopoly Theory: Some Examples", *Journal of Industrial Economics* 32 (Sept 1983) pp 97–110.

[16] Bresnahan, T., "Duopoly Models with Consistent Conjectures", *American Economic Review,* 71 pp 934–45 (Dec 1981).

[17] Brozen, Yale, "Bain's concentration and rates of return revisited", *Journal of Law and Economics,* 14 (October), pp 351–70 (1970).

[18] Brozen, Yale, "The Persistence of "High Rates of Return" in Very Stable Concentration Industries", *Journal of Law and Economics,* 14 pp 501 (1971).

[19] Buxton, A.J., S.W. Davies and B.R. Lyons, "Concentration and Advertising in Consumer and Product Markets", *The Journal of Industrial Economics,* 32 (4), pp 451–65 (1984).

[20] Cable, J.R. and P. Steer, "Internal Organisation and Profit: an Empirical Analysis of large UK companies", *Journal of Industrial Economics,* 27, 13–30

[21] Cady, J., "Advertising Restrictions and Retail Prices", *Journal of Advertising Research,* 16 pp 27–30 (1976).

[22] Carroll, Lewis, *Through the Looking Glass,* Collins (Library of Classics Series) London (1897).

[23] Caves, R.E., M.E. Porter and A.M. Spence, with J.T.Scott, *Competition in the Open Economy: A Model applied to Canada,* Cambridge, Mass. Harvard University Press, 1980.
[24] Caves, R.E. and B.S. Yamey, "Risk and Corporate Rates of Return: Comment", *Quarterly Journal of Economics,* 85, pp 513–17 (1971).
[25] Caves, R.E. and M. Porter, "From Entry Barriers to Mobility Barriers", *Quarterly Journal of Economics,* 91 (1), pp 421–34 (1977).
[26] Caves, R.E. and M. Uekusa, *Industrial Organisation in Japan,* Washington, D.C.: Brookings Institution, 1976.
[27] Chamberlin, E.H., *The Theory of Monopolistic Competition,* Eight edition 1962, Cambridge Mass,: Harvard University Press, 1933.
[28] Chandler, A.D. Jr., *Strategy and Structure: Chapters in the History of Industrial Enterprise,* Cambridge, Mass. MIT Press, 1962.
[29] Cheng, L., "Comparing Bertrand and Cournot Equilibria: a Geometric Approach", *Rand Journal of Economics,* 16, Spring 1985, pp 146-52.
[30] Clark, J.B., *The Control of Trusts,* New York: Macmillan 1902.
[31] Clark, J.M., "Towards a Theory of Workable Competition", *American Economic Review,* 30, (June 1940), pp 241–56.
[32] Clark, J.M., *Competition as a Dynamic Process,* Washington, DC, Brookings Institution, 1961.
[33] Clark, K.B., "Unionisation and Firm Performance: The Impact on Profits Growth and Productivity", *American Economic Review,* 74 (1984) pp 893–919.
[34] Clarke, D.G., "Econometric Measurement of the Duration of Advertising Effects on Sales", *Journal of Marketing Research,* 13, pp 345–357 (1976).
[35] Clarke, R., *Industrial Economics,* Oxford: Basil Blackwell, 1985. [36] Clarke, R. and S. Davies, "Market Structure and Price-Cost Margins", *Economica,* 49 (3) pp 277–88 (1982).
[37] Clarke, R., S. Davies and M. Waterson, "The Profitability-Concentration Relation: Market Power or Efficiency?", *Journal of Industrial Economics,* 32 (4), pp 435–50 (1984).
[38] Collins, N.R. and L.E. Preston, *Concentration and Price-Cost Margins in Manufacturing Industries,* Berkeley: University of California Press 1968.
[39] Collins, N.R. and L.E. Preston, "Price-cost margins and industry structure", *Review of Economics and Statistics,* 51, pp 271–86 (1969).
[40] Comanor, W., and T. Wilson. "Advertising, Market Structure, and Performance", *Review of Economics and Statistics,* 49 (4), pp 423–40 (1967).
[41] Comanor, W.S. and T.A. Wilson, "The Effect of Advertising on Competition: A Survey", *Journal of Economic Literature,* 17, pp 453–76 (1979).
[42] Connolly, R.A. and M. Hirschey, "R&D, Market Structure and Profits: A Value-based Approach", Review of Economics and Statistics, 66, pp 682– (1984).
[43] Cootner, Paul and D. Holland, "Rate of Return and Business Risk", *Bell Journal or Economics and Management Science.* 1(Autumn), pp 211–26 (1970).
[44] Cournot, A., *Researchers into the Mathemetical Principles of the Theory of Wealth,* New York: Macmillan, 1927.
[45] Cowling, K., (ed), *Market Structure and Corporate Behaviour* London: Gray-Mills, 1972.
[46] Cowling, K., "On the Theoretical Specification of Structure—Performance Relations", *European Economic Review,* 8 (1), pp 1–14 (1976).
[47] Cowling, K., and M. Waterson, "Price-Cost Margins and Market Structure", *Economica,* 43 (3), pp 267–74 (1976).
[48] Cubbin, J.S., "A Measure of Apparent Collusion in Oligopoly", *Warwick Economic Research Paper,* no 49, (1974) (out of print).

[49] Cubbin, J.S., "Quality Change and Pricing Behaviour in the UK Car Indsutry", 1956–68, *Economica,* February, 43–58 (1975).

[50] Cubbin, J.S., "Apparent Collusion and Conjectural Variations in Differentiated Oligopoly", *International Journal of Industrial Organisation,* June, (vol 1), pp 155–64 (1983).

[51] Cubbin, J.S. and S. Domberger, "Advertising and Post-entry Oligopoly Behaviour", mimeo, London Business School, 1987.

[52] Cubbin, J.S. and P. Geroski, "The Convergence of Profits in the Long Run: Inter-firm and Inter-industry Comparisons", *Journal of Industrial Economics,* 25, pp 427–442 (June 1987).

[53] Cubbin, J.S. and G. Hall, "Directors' Remuneration in the Theory of the Firm: Specification and Testing of the Managerial Hypothesis, *European Economic Review,* pp 333–48 (1983).

[54] Cubbin, J.S. and D. Leech, "Growth Versus Profit Maximization: a Simultaneous Equations Approach to Testing the Marris Model", *Managerial and Decision Economics,* 7, pp 123–32 (June 1986).

[55] Cubbin, J.S. and T. Tsitouras, "Why do firms Choose Prices?", mimeo, Queen Mary College, Department of Economics, University of London 1987.

[56] Curry, B. and K.D. George, "Industrial Concentration: A Survey", *Journal of Industrial Economics* 31, pp 203–55 (1983).

[57] Dalton, and Penn, "The Concentration-Profitability Relationship: Is There a Critical Concentration Ratio?, *Journal of Industrial Economics* 25, pp 133–42 (1976).

[58] Dansby, R.E. and R.D. Willig, "Industry Performance Gradient Indexes", *American Economic Review,* 69, pp 249–60 (1979).

[59] Davies, S. "Minimum Efficient Size and Seller Concentration: an Empirical Problem", *Journal of Industrial Economics,* 28 (3), pp 287–302 (1980).

[60] Davis, E., "Express Coaching Since 1980: Liberalisation in Practice", *Fiscal Studies,* 1984.

[61] Demsetz, Harold, "Industry Structure, Market Rivalry and Public Policy",. *Journal of Law and Economics,* 16, pp 1–10 (April 1973).

[62] Demsetz, Harold, "Two Systems of Belief about Monopoly", *Industrial Concentration: The New Learning,* H. Goldschmid, H. Mann and J. Weston (eds.), Little Brown, Boston, 1974.

[63] Dixit, A.K., "A Model of Duopoly Suggesting a Theory of Entry Barriers", *Bell Journal of Economics,* 10 Spring, pp 20–32 (1979).

[64] Dixit, A.K., "The Role of Investment in Entry Deterrence", *Economic Journal,* 90, pp 95–106 (1980).

[65] Domberger, S., *Industrial Structure, Pricing and Inflation,* Martin Robertson, Oxford 1983.

[66] Domowitz, I., G.R. Hubbard and B.C. Peterson, "Business Cycles and the Relationship between Concentration and Price-cost Margins", *Rand Journal of Economics,* 17 (1), pp 1–17 (1986).

[67] Dorfman, R. and P. O. Steiner, "Optimal Advertising and Optimal Quality", *American Economic Review,* 44, pp 826–36 (1954).

[68] Dowrick, S., "Bargaining and Income Distribution in UK Manufacturing".

[69] Eichner, A., *The Emergence of Oligopoly: Sugar Refining as a Case Study.*

[70] Encoua, D. and A. Jacquemin, "Degree of Monopoly, Indices of Concentration and Threat of Entry", *International Economic Review,* 21, pp 87–105 (1980)

[71] Encoua, D. and Jacquemin, A. (1982) Organisational Efficiency and Monopoly Power. *European Economic Review,* 19 (1982) 25–51.

[72] Farber, S., "Buyer Market Structure and R&D Effect: A Simultaneous Equations

Model", *Review of Economics and Statistics,* 63 pp 336–45 (1981).
[73] Firth, M., "The Profitability of Takeovers and Mergers", *Economic Journal,* 89, pp 316–28 (1979).
[74] Fisher, F.M. and J.J., "McGowan Advertising and Welfare: Comment", *Bell Journal of Economics,* 10, pp 726–9 (1979).
[75] Fisher, F.M. and J.J. McGowan, "On the Misuse of Accounting Rates of Return to Inter Monopoly Profits", *American Economic Journal,* 73, pp 82–87 (1983).
[76] Fisher, I.N. and G.R. Hall, "Risk and Corporate Rates of Return, *Quarterly Journal of Economics,* 83 pp 79–92 (1969).
[77] Fouraker, L.E. and S. Siegel, *Bargaining Behaviour,* New York: McGraw-Hill (1963).
[78] Fudenberg, D. and J. Tirole, *Dynamic Models of Oligopoly* London: Harwood, 1986.
[79] Fuss, M.A. and U.K. Gupta, "A Cost Functions Approach to the Estimation of Miniumum Efficient Scale", *European Economic Review,* 15, pp 125–35 (1981).
[80] Gale, B.T., "Market Share and Rate of Return", *Review of Economics and Statistics,* 54 pp 412–33 (November 1972).
[81] George, K.D. and T.S. Ward, *The Structure of Industry in the EEC,* Cambridge: Cambridge University Press, 1975.
[82] Geroski, P., "Simultaneous Equations Models of the Structure-Performance Paradigm", *European Economic Review,* 19 (1) pp 145–58 (1982).
[83] Goldschmid, H.J., (ed), *Business Disclosure: Government's Need to Know* New York, McGraw-Hill, 1979.
[84] Goldschmid, H. and H.M. Mann, "Repetition and Price Levels in the Retail Gasoline Market". *Review of Economics and Statistics,* 60, pp 252–58 (May).
[85] Goto, "Business Groups in a Market Economy", *European Economic Review.* (1982).
[86] Grabowski, H.G. and D.C. Mueller, "Industrial Research and Development Intangible Capital Stocks, and Firm Profit Rates", *Bell Journal of Economics,* 9, pp 328–343 (1978).
[87] Grant, R.M. "Pricing Behaviour in the UK Wholesale Market for Petrol 1970–1980: A Structure Conduct Analysis", *Journal of Industrial Economics* 30 pp 271–292 (March 1982).
[88] Green, E.J. and R.H. Porter, "Noncooperative Collusion under Imperfect Price Information", *Econometrica* 49, pp 87–100, (November 1984).
[89] Greer, D.F. "Advertising and Market Concentration", *Southern Economic Journal,* (1967) 38 pp 10–32 (July 1971).
[90] Haid, A. and M. Neumann, "Market Share and Concentration in the Structure Performance Paradigm and the New Hearing: A Critical Appraisal", mimeo, University of Erlangen—Nuernberg.
[91] Hall, M. and L. Weiss, "Firm Size and Profitability", *Review of Economics & Statistics,* 49, pp 319–331.
[92] Hannah, L. and J.A. Kay, *Concentration in Modern Industry,* London, Macmillan (1977).
[93] Harcourt, G., "The Accountant in a Golden Age". *Oxford Economic Papers,* 17 pp 66–80 (March 1965).
[94] Hart, P.E. and R. Clarke, *Concentration in British Industry: 1935–75,* Cambridge: Cambridge University Press 1980.
[95] Hart, P.E. and E. Morgan, "Market Structure and Economic Performance in the United Kingdom", *Journal of Industrial Economics,* 25, pp 177–93 (1977).
[96] Holl, P., "Effect of Control Type on the Performance of the Firm in the UK". *Journal of Industrial Economics,* 23, pp 1257–71 (June 1977).

[97] Hurdle, G.A., "Leverage, Risk, Market Structure and Profitability", *Review of Economics and Statistics,* 54 pp 412–23 (November 1974).
[98] Imel, B. and P. Helmberger, "Estimation of Structure-Profit Relationships with Application to the Food Processing Sector", *American Economic Review,* pp 614–27 (September 1971).
[99] Ireland, N., *Product Differentiation and Non-price Competition,* Oxford: Basil Blackwell, 1987.
[100] Jacquemin, A., *The New Industrial Organisation,* Oxford, Clarenden Press, 1987.
[101] Jacquemin, A. and H. DeJong *European Industrial Organisation,* London: Macmillan (1977).
[102] Jacquemin, A., E. Ghellinck and C. Huveneers, "Concentration and Profitability in a Small Open Economy", *Journal of Industrial Economics,* 29, pp 131–144.
[103] Jenny, F., "Wage Rates, Concentration and Unionisation in French Manufacturing Industries", *Journal of Industrial Economics,* 26, pp 315–327 (June 1978).
[104] Jenny, F. and A.P. Weber, "Profit Rates and Structural Variables in French Manufacturing Industries", *European Economic Review,* 7, 187–206 (1976).
[105] Jensen, M.C., "Capital Market: Theory and Evidence". *Bell Journal of Economics and Management Science,* 3, pp 357–98 (Autumn 1972).
[106] Kamien, M.I. and N.L. Schwartz, "Conjectural Variations", *Canadian Journal of Economics,* 16(2) pp 191–211 (May 1983).
[107] Kay, J., "Accountants too could be Happy in a Golden Age: the Accountant's Rate of Profit and the Internal Rate of Return", *Oxford Economic Papers,* 28 pp 447–60 (November 1976).
[108] Kay, J. and C Mayer, "On the Application of Accounting Rates of Return", *Economical Journal,* 96, pp 199–207 pp(1986).
[109] Kreps, D.M. and R. Wilson, "Sequential Equilibria", *Econometrica,* 50 (4), pp 863–94 (1982)a.
[110] Kwoka, J. "Does the Choice of Concentration Measure Really Matter?", *Journal of Industrial Economies,* 20, pp 445-53 (1980).
[111] Lamm, R.M., "Prices and Concentration in the Food Retailing Industry", *Journal or Industrial Economics,* 30, pp 67-78 (1981).
[112] Lancaster, K., "A New Approach to Consumer Theory", *Journal of Political Economy,* 74, pp 132–157 (1966).
[113] Lancaster, K., *Variety, Equity and Efficiency,* Oxford: Basil Blackwell, (1979).
[114] Leamer, E.E., "Model Choice and Specification Analysis in Z Griliches and M D Intrilligator", eds. *Handbook of Econometrics,* Vol 2 Amsterdam: North Holland, (1983).
[115] Lerner, A.P., "The Concept of Monopoly and the Measurement of Monopoly Power", *Review of Economic Studies,* 1, pp 157–75 (1934).
[116] Liebowitz, S.J., "What do Census Price-cost Margins Measure?", *Journal of Law and Economics,* 25(2).
[117] Liesner, H., (Committee Chairman), *A Review of Monopolies and Mergers Policy,* London: HMSO.
[118] Lindenberg, E.B. and S.A. Ross, "Tobin's q ratio and Industrial Organisation", *Journal of Business,* 54 (1), pp 1–32 (1981).
[119] Lintner, J., "The Valuation of Risk Assets and the Selection of Risky Investments in Stock Portfolio and Capital Budgets", *Review of Economics and Statistics,* 47, pp 13–37 (1965).
[120] Long, W.F., "Market Share, Concentration and Profits: Intra Industry and Industry Evidence", unpublished, US Federal Trade Commission, 1980.
[121] Mann, H.M., "Seller Concentration, Barriers to Entry, and Rates of Return in

Thirty Industries", *Review of Economics and Statistics,* 48, pp 296–307 (August 1966).

[122] Marion, B.W., W.F. Mueller, et. al. "The Profit and Performance of Leading Food Chains 1970–74", (Study for the Joint Economic Committee of the U.S. Congress) *Government Printing Office,* Washington, D.C. (1977).

[123] Markowitz, M., "The Utility of Wealth", *Journal of Political Economy* 60(2) pp 151–8 (April 1952).

[124] Marris, R., *The Economic Theory of Managerial Capitilism,* London: Macmillan 1964.

[125] Martin, S., "Advertising, Concentration and Profitability: the Simultaneity Problem", *Bell Journal of Economics,* 10, pp 639–47 (1979).

[126] Marvel, H.P., "Competition and Price Levels in the Retail Gasoline Market", *Review of Economics and Statistics,* 60, pp 252–58 (May 1978).

[127] Mason, E.S., "Price and Production Policies of Large Scale Enterprise", *American Economic Review Supplement,* 29 pp 61–74 (March 1939).

[128] Meeks, G., *Disappointing Marriage: A Study of the Gains from Mergers,* Cambridge University Press, England (1977).

[129] Mueller, D., "The Persistence of Profits Above the Norm". *Economica,* 44, pp 369–80 (1977).

[130] Mueller, D., *The Determinants and Effects of Mergers: An International Comparison,* Cambridge: Oelgeschleger, Funn and Hain (1980).

[131] Mueller, D., *Profits in the Long Run,* Cambridge, England, Cambridge University Press (1986).

[132] Mueller, W.F. and R.T. Rogers, "The Role of Advertising in Changing Concentration in Manufacturing Industries", *Review of Economics and Statistics,* 12 pp 89–96 (1980).

[133] Muller, J., "The Impact of Mergers on Concentration: A Study of Eleven West German Industries", *Journal of Industrial Economics,* 25, pp 113–32 (Dec 1976).

[134] Neumann, M.B. and A. Haid, "Profitability, Risk and Market Structure in West Germany", *Journal of Industrial Economics* 27 pp 227–42 (1979).

[135] Neumann, M and A. Haid, "Market Share and Concentration in the Structure Performance Paradigm and the New Learning: A Critical Appraisal", mimeo: University of Erlangen–Nuernberg.

[136] Newman, H.H. "Strategic Groups and the Structure Performance Relationship", *Review of Economics and Statistics,* 60, 417–27 (1978).

[137] Nordaus, *Invention, Growth and Welfare,* Cambridge: MIT Press (1969).

[138] Osborne, D.K., "The Role of Entry in Oligopoly Theory", Journal Of Political Economy, 72 pp 396–402 (August 1964).

[139] Pagouletos, E. and R. Sorenson, "A Simultaneous Equation Analysis of Advertising, Concentration and Profitability", *Southern Economic Journal* 47, pp 728–41 (1981).

[140] Palmer, J., "The Profit-performance Effects of the Separation of Ownership from Control in Large US Industrial Corporations", *Bell Journal of Economics,* 4 pp 292–303 (1973).

[141] Penn,

[142] Phillips, A., "An Econometric Study of Price-fixing in Market Structure and Performance in the early 1950s" in Cowling, K., (ed) *Market Structure and Corporate Behaviour.*

[143] Phillips, A., "A Critique of Empirical Studies of Relations between Market Structure and Profitability", *Journal of Industrial Economics,* 24 (2) pp 214–9 (1976).

[144] Phlips, L., *Effects of Industrial Concentration: A Cross Sectional Analysis for the Common Market,* Amsterdam, North-Holland (1973).

[145] Pindyck, *Journal of Law and Economics,* 28 pp 193–222 (1985).

[146] Porter, M.E., "Consumer Behaviour, Retailer Power, and Market Performance in Consumer Goods Industries", *Review of Economics and Statistics,* pp 419–36 (Nov 1974).

[147] Posner, R., *Antitrusthaw: An Economic Perspective,* Chicago: 1976.

[148] Pratten, G.F., *Economies of Scale in Manufacturing Industry* Cambridge: Cambridge University Press (1971).

[149] Qualls, D. "Concentration, Barriers to Entry and Long run Economic Profit Margins", *Journal of Industrial Economics* 12pp.146-68 (April 1972).

[150] Ravenscraft, D.J., "Structure-Profit-Relationships at the Line of Business Level", *Review of Economics and Statistics,* 65, pp 22-31 (1983).

[151] Reekie, W.D., "Advertising and Market Structure: Another Approach", *Economic Journal* 85 pp 165-74 (March 1985).

[152] Reekie, W.D., *Advertising and Price,* London: Advertising Association, 1979.

[153] Rhoades, S.A., "Structure-Performance Studies in Banking an updated Summary and Evaluation", *Federal Reserve Board Staff Studies 119* (1982).

[154] Robinson, J., *The Economics of Imperfect Competition* London: Macmillan 1934.

[155] Rosenthele, Hon Benjamin, "Retail Prescription Drug Prices", *US Congress House Document,* Washington 1973.

[156] Salinger, M.A., "Tobin's Q, Unionisation and the Concentration—profits Relationship",. *Rand Journal of Economics* 15 pp 159-70 (Summer 1984).

[157] Salop, S., "Strategic Entry Deterrence", *American Economic Review,* (Papers and Proceedings) 69, pp 335-8 (1979).

[158] Sampson, J. Untraced Mimeo.

[159] Sargant, F.P., *The Logic of Industrial Organisation,* London: Routledge and Kegan Paul, 1933.

[160] Schelling, T.C., *The Strategy of Conflict* Oxford: Oxford University Press (1960).

[161] Scherer, F.M., *Industrial Structure and Market Performance,* Chicago: Ron McNally, 2nd Edition, 1980.

[162] Schmalensee, R.,"Economics of Scale and Barriers to Entry", *Journal of Political Economy,* 89: pp 1228-1238 (1981).

[163] Schmalensee, R., "Do Markets Differ Much?", *American Economic Review,* 75, pp 341-351 (1985).

[164] Schmalensee, R., "Collusion Versus Differential Efficiency: Testing Alternative Hypothesis", *Journal of Industrial Economics,* 35 pp 399-426 (June 1987).

[165] Schmalensee, R., "Inter-industry Studies of Structure and Performance", in R Schmalensee and R Willig (eds) *Handbook of Industrial Economics,* Amsterdam: North Holland. In Press 1987.

[166] Sharpe, W., "Capital Asset Prices: a Theory of Market Equilibrium Under Condition of Risk". *Journal of Finance,* 19 pp.425-42 (September 1964).

[167] Shaw, R.W. and P. Simpson, "The Persistence of Monopoly: An Investigation of the Effectiveness of the United Kingdom Monopolies Commission", Journal of Industrial Economies, 24 pp 355-72 (June 1986).

[168] Shepherd, W.G. "The Elements of Market Structure", *Review of Economics and Statistics,* 39 pp.25-38 (1972).

[169] Shepherd, W.G., *The Economics of Industrial Organisation,* Englewood Cliffs, NJ, Prentice-Hall, 1979.

[170] Spence, M., "Entry Capacity, Investment and Oligopoly Pricing", *Bell Journal of Economics,* 8 pp 534-44 (1977).

[171] Stauffer, Thomas R., "The Measurement of Corporate Rates of Return: a Generalised Formulation", *Bell Journal of Economics and Management Science,* 2 pp 434-69 (Autumn 1971)

[172] Stigler, E.J., "Extent and Basis of Monopoly", *American Economic Review,* 32, (194) supp, 2-3.

[173] Stigler, G.J., "A Theory of Oligopoly", *Journal of Political Economy,* 72 (1), pp 44-61 (1964).

[174] Stigler, G.J., *The Organisation of Industry,* R.O. Irwin, Homewood, Ill. (1968).

[175] Stigler, G.J. and Kindahl, *The Behaviour of Industrial Prices,* New York: Columbia, University Press, 1970.

[176] Stiglitz and Matthewson, *New Development in the Analysis of Market Structure,* Cambridge, Mass. MIT Press, 1985.

[177] Strickland, A. and L. Weiss, "Advertising Concentration and Price-Cost Margins". *Journal of Political Economy,* 84 (5) pp 1109–1121 (1976).

[178] Sullivan, T.G., "The Cost of Capital at the Market Power of Firms", *Review of Economics and Statistics,* 60 pp 209–17 (1978).

[179] Sutton, C.J., "Advertising, Concentration and Competition", *Economic Journal,* 84, pp 56–69 (1974).

[180] Sylos-Labini, P.,*Oligopoly and Technical Progress,* Cambridge, Mass, Harvard University Press, 1962.

[181] Thompson, R.S., "Structure and Conduct in Local Advertising Markets: the Case of Irish, Provincial Newspapers", *Journal of Industrial Economics,* 28 (2), pp 241–9 (1984).

[182] Walshe, G., *Recent Trends in Monopoly in Great Britain* Cambridge: Cambridge University Press (1974).

[183] Waterson, M., *Economic Theory of the Industry* Cambridge, England, Cambridge University Press, 1984.

[184] Weiss, L.W., "Advertising, Profits and Corporate Taxes", *Review of Economics and Statistics,* 51, pp 421–430 (1969).

[185] Weiss, L.W., "Concentration and Labour Earnings", *American Economic Review,* 56 (1) pp 96–117 (March 1966).

[186] Weiss, L.W., "Factors in Changing Concentration", *Review of Economics and Statistics,* 45, pp 70–77 (1963).

[187] Weiss, L.W., "The Concentration—Profits Relationship and Antitrust" *Industrial Concentration: The New Learning,* (1974).

[188] Weiss, L.W., "Quantitive Studies of Industrial Organisation, Frontiers of Quantative Economics", M. Intrilligator (ed.), North-Holland, Amsterdam, 1971.

[189] von Weizsacher, C., "A Welfare Analysis of Barriers to Entry", *Bell Journal of Economics and Management Science,* 11 pp 399– 420 (1980).

[190] White, L., "Searching for the Critical Concentration Ratio: An Application of the Switching of Regimes Technique", *Studies in Non-Linear Estimation,* S. Goldfed and R. Quandt (eds.). Ballinger, Boston (1976).

[191] Williamson, O.E., *Markets and Hierarchies,* New York, Macmillan, 1975.

[192] Winn, D., "On the Relations Between Rate of Return, Risk and Market Structure", *Quarterly Journal of Economics,* 91 pp 157–63 (1977).

INDEX

Accounting data 32, 35–39
Advertising 37–38, 55
Allard, R.J. 34
Axelrod, R. 13–14

Bain, Joe S 4–6, 20, 35, 47, 53, 57
Baker, Samuel H. 33
Barriers to Entry 19–24, 41, 49, 53, 68
Baumol, W.J. 24
Bertrand model 14
Bobel, I 62
Boston Consultancy Group (BCG) 22
Bothwell, J.L. 63
Brozen Yale 53, 64
Business cycles 62

Cable, John R 25
Capital Asset Pricing Model 33
Caves, Richard 33, 47–48, 52, 54
Census data 41
Chamberlin, E.H. 4, 16, 49
Chandler, Alfred D 25
Clark, J.B. 2
Clark, J.M. 2
Collins, N.R. 41, 55
Comamor, William S 47, 54
Company data 40
Connolly, R.A. 56
Cooley, T.F. 63
Corporate Structure 25
Concentration 45, 49, 52, 57, 67
Contestable Markets 24
Cost advantages 20–22
Cost of Capital 32, 35, 41
Cournot model 9, 11, 14, 67

Cowling, Keith 9–11, 58
Cubbin, John 32

Dansby R.E. 7
Data quality 59
Demand advantages 54
Demsetz, H. 59
Depreciation 37–39, 41
Domberger, Simon 62
Domowitz, I. 62

Econometric problems 42
Economies of scale 53
Efficiency hypothesis 59, 66
Encoua, David 7
Engineering approach 46
Entry Barriers 19–24, 41, 49, 53, 68
Excess capacity 21

Farber, S 62
Federal Trade Commission 30
Firm-specific factors 24–26
Fisher, F.M. 35–36
Fisher, I.N. 33
Fudenberg, D. 6
Fuss, M.A. 47

George, Kenneth D 47
Geroski, Paul 56, 57
Grabowski, H. 26
Green, E.J. 14, 62
Gupta, U.K. 47

Haid, A 61,62
Hall, Graham 32

Hall, G.R. 33
Hall, T.E. 63
Hannah, Leslie 48
Harcourt, G 35
Hart, P 47, 58
Helmberger, P 40
Hirschey, M 56
Hubbard, G.R. 62
Hurdle, G.A. 33

Imel, B 40
Industry: Definition 4, 27–29
Internal Rate of Return 35–36
Ireland, Norman 16

Jacquemin, Alexis 7

Kamien, M. 15
Kay, John 35, 48

Lamm, R.M. 53
Lerner index 8, 10, 17, 18
Lerner index vs. rate of return 8–9, 18
Liebowitz, S.J. 55
Line of business (LB) data 31, 62–63
Lintner, J. 33
Long, W.F. 36

McGowan, J.J. 35–36
Market Share 10, 23, 61
Market Structure 45
Markowitz, M. 33
Marris, Robin 38
Martin, S. 36
Measurement error 43
Mergers 48, 59, 67
Methodology 5–6
Minimum efficient scale 46
Morgan, E. 58
Mueller, D. 26, 48, 57, 65
Müller, J.
Multicollinearity 44, 51
Multidivisional (M-form) structure 25

Neumann, M. 61, 62
Newman, H.H. 24

Oligopoly theory 9–19
Ownership and Control 25

Pareto optimality 7
Peterson, B.C. 62
Performance 3, 7–9, 55, 58
Persistence of profitability 64–5
Phillips, Almarin 56
PIMS (Profit Impact of Marketing Strategy) 29–30
Policy implications 67
Porter, R.H. 14, 62
Posner, R. 27
Pratten, C. 46
Preston, L.E. 41, 55
Price-cost margins 41, 62
Price flexibility 16, 62–63
Price behaviour vs. quantity setting 16
Pricing strategies 22
Prisoners' Dilemma 13, 16
Product Differentiation 49–50
Profitability 52, 55, 68

Q ratio 38
Qualls, D. 57

Ravenscraft, D.J. 36, 62
Risk 3, 39
Robinson, Joan 16

Sample Selection 5, 58
Salop, S. 21
Sampson, J. 35
Schelling, T.C. 20
Schmalensee, Richard 63, 65
Schwartz, Nancy 15
Sharpe, W. 33
Shepherd, W.G. 4
Simulations equations 42, 51, 56
Specification error 43
Stigler, George J 2, 16, 20, 23, 62
Strategic groups 24
Sullivan, T.G. 34
Strickland, A. 47, 51
Structure-Conduct-Performance framework 3, 58

Taxation 40, 55
Taxicabs 21
Thompson, R.S. 53
TIT FOR TAT strategy 13–14, 17
Tobin, J. 38
Tyrole, J. 6

Unionisation 57

Wages 57
Walshe, G. 48
Waterson, Michael 9–11, 58
Weiss, L. 47, 51
Williamson, Oliver E. 25
Willig, R.D. 7
Winn, D. 33
Workable competition 2–3
Wilson, T.A. 47, 54

Yamey, B. 33

www.ingramcontent.com/pod-product-compliance
Lightning Source LLC
LaVergne TN
LVHW021114300926
849160LV00009B/729
* 9 7 8 0 4 1 5 8 6 6 0 6 4 *